MS-DOS® 6.0

© Educational Systems, Incorporated, Northbrook, Illinois 60062

Printed in the U.S.A.

ACKNOWLEDGMENTS

MICROREF® is a registered trademark of Educational Systems, Inc. **MS-DOS®** is a registered trademark of Microsoft Corp. Educational Systems, Inc. is not affiliated with Microsoft Corp., nor was it authorized by Microsoft Corp. to write this Guide.

Published by:
Educational Systems, Inc. • 706 Landwehr Road
Northbrook, Illinois 60062 • (708) 498-3780

Welcome to the world of DOS! MS-DOS® is an operating system that runs on IBM PC® and PC-compatible microcomputers. The operating system is a necessary part of any computer. Your computer needs DOS (Disk Operating System) to use its various components such as disk drives, keyboard, monitor, memory, modem, and printer.

MICROREF® is the MICROcomputer user's comprehensive quick REFerence guide to popular business software. Use MICROREF as a reference and learning aid along with your other reference and training materials. The following MICROREF features will help you save time and use DOS to your best advantage.

- **TABLE OF CONTENTS**
- **PROCEDURES**
- **ALPHABETICAL LISTS OF COMMANDS AND EXAMPLES**
- ☑ **CHECKLIST OF IMPORTANT COMMANDS**
- **GLOSSARY**
- **INDEX**

Use MICROREF in the way that is most effective for you. You might review an entire group of procedures before you begin certain tasks. Or, use the examples as "memory refreshers." In any case, use MICROREF often...and soon you will be working comfortably and effectively with your operating system!

DOS Function Keys

	F1	F2	F3	F4	F5	F6	F7	F8	F9	F10	F11	F12
ALT							Clear Commands			Clear Macros		
	Copy Next Character	Copy to a Character	Rest of Characters	Skip to Character	Stop Startup/ Retype	^Z End of File	Redisplay Commands	Step Startup/ Search	Reissue a Command			

* Color keys are available when the Doskey program is installed.

TABLE OF CONTENTS

Table of Contents

GETTING STARTED

DOS VERSIONS

Guidelines
- Use this guide if your IBM PC® or PC-compatible computer is running MS-DOS 6.0.
- Some commands may work for previous versions of DOS.
- For a list of when new commands were introduced in DOS, see pages 102–104.

View DOS Version
1. To view the version of DOS currently installed on your computer, type **VER** and press ENTER

DOS Procedures: Steps and Options
In this guide, DOS procedures consist of steps numbered in the order in which they are to be performed. Whenever you have a choice of what to do next, a bullet (■) precedes each option.

DOS 6.0
DOS 6.0 is an updated version of the popular MS-DOS operating system.

Compatibility: All previous DOS commands and their syntax still work in DOS 6.0

Upgraded: DOS 6.0 adds new features to familiar DOS commands.

New: DOS 6.0 provides completely new commands as well.

New Installation Process

The Setup program asks you for information while you install DOS 6.0 on your computer. The new version will replace the current version of DOS. As a backup, the installation program creates an Uninstall floppy disk.

1. Format a disk that is compatible with Drive A: and label the disk "Uninstall Disk." For information on formatting a disk, see page 49.
2. a. To begin installation, place Disk 1 in Drive A: or B:
   b. Type that drive name (**A:** or **B:**) and press **ENTER**
3. ▪ To install DOS 6.0 on a hard disk, type **SETUP** and press **ENTER**, or
   ▪ To install DOS 6.0 on a floppy disk, type **SETUP** /F and press **ENTER**, or
   ▪ For a special installation of DOS 6.0, see the optional switches at right. You can combine switches in one command (e.g., **SETUP** /F /B).
4. Follow the instructions on the screen. If you need help at any point, press **F1**. Note: You have a choice of installing Backup, Undelete, and Anit-Virus programs for Windows and MS-DOS, Windows only, MS-DOS only, or None. To change which versions of the programs to install, highlight program (e.g., Backup) and press **ENTER** to select versions. To use these programs in DOS, install them for either Windows and MS-DOS or for MS-DOS only.
5. When you are finished, your computer should be running DOS 6.0. If it has a problem booting, insert the "Uninstall Disk" in Drive A: and restart your computer. This runs the original operating system.
6. To have DOS reconfigure your CONFIG.SYS and AUTOEXEC.BAT files to optimize memory usage, run the **MEMMAKER** command on page 88

Optional Switches for SETUP Command

SETUP /B	(displays black and white setup screen instead of color)
SETUP /E	(installs expanded version including Windows and other optional programs, otherwise you are prompted during setup if you want these programs)
SETUP /F	(installs on floppy disk with minimal number of DOS files)
SETUP /I	(does not try to detect your hardware before Installing)
SETUP /M	(installs a minimal number of DOS files)
SETUP /Q	(copies files automatically to a hard disk)
SETUP /U	(installs even if it detects incompatible disk partition)

Install DOS 6.0

How Has DOS Improved in Version 6.0?

Hardware Detection: DOS is a little "smarter" now. It can sense more of what is happening inside the hardware. A virus checker can seek out dangerous viruses on your drives and in your computer's memory. A file defragmenter utility can read how your drive stores its files and recombine files into contiguous locations. An enhanced SMARTDRV.EXE driver can speed up disk usage. A POWER command relieves the strain on battery powered computers. And a diagnostics program can help you evaluate your hardware by displaying your computer's setup and hardware on the screen.

Better Memory Management: DOS's new MEMMAKER program, enhanced LOADHIGH and DEVICEHIGH commands, and enhanced EMM386.EXE driver can improve your computer's use of available memory. View more detailed information with the MEM command.

Disk Compression: Increase hard disk size with DBLSPACE.

Simplified Moving, Renaming, Deleting, and Undeleting: You can move files without having to copy them first, then delete the originals (MOVE). You can rename directories without having to create new directories (MOVE). You can delete entire directories and their subdirectories with one command (DELTREE). And by replacing the MIRROR command with more UNDELETE switches, DOS enables you to select from one of three deletion protection schemes.

Multiple Configurations: Now your computer can have multiple personalities. You can halt or step the CONFIG.SYS file or halt the AUTOEXEC.BAT program during booting (F5 and F8 keys). Depending on what type of programs you want to run during a given session, you can select from different preset boot options in your CONFIG.SYS and AUTOEXEC.BAT programs (see pages 84–87). In addition, you can prompt the user of a batch file to select from several choices of action (CHOICE).

New DOS and Windows Utilities: If you need to undelete files, back up files, or remove viruses, DOS 6.0 provides new menu-driven programs in either DOS or Windows to simplify your work.

Link to Other Computers: Use INTERLNK and INTERSVR to link to another computer, such as a laptop, via a serial or parallel port. This is a way to copy files between computers, to run a program on another computer, or to use another computer's printer.

More Help: The HELP command gives you menu-driven support.

STARTING AND EXITING

Guidelines

- Before you start up your computer, make sure that you can "boot" (bootstrap) your computer. That is, you must give your computer the information it needs to start and to recognize its components.

- If you have a floppy disk system, make sure you have a boot disk (also called a System Disk or DOS Disk). This disk contains the Disk Operating System, a collection of files that you must load into your computer's memory before you load any other files.

- If you have a hard disk system, you can either boot your computer with a boot disk or boot directly from your hard disk. Normally you boot directly from the hard disk. If your hard disk is corrupted or will not boot, you can boot from a floppy disk. Make sure that you have a floppy boot disk on hand in case this happens to you.

- To create a boot disk, see **CREATING BOOT DISKS** on page 72.

- Before you shut down your computer, save files and close applications (programs). Not doing so will cause you to lose your work and could damage open applications.

Start Up Your Computer
Use this procedure if the power switch on your computer is off.

1. ■ If you wish to boot with a floppy boot disk, insert boot disk into Drive A: (label up, notch on left) and close the drive door, or
   ■ If you wish to boot from a hard disk, remove all floppy disks from disk drives and leave drive doors open
2. Turn on computer (see computer reference material if necessary)
3. If prompted for a Startup Menu choice, either type the number of the choice (e.g., **2**) or move the highlighted bar to the choice. Then press **ENTER**.
4. a. If prompted for a date:
      ■ If displayed date is correct, press **ENTER**, or
      ■ Type current date (e.g., 8–11–93) and press **ENTER**
   b. If prompted for time (24-hour clock):
      ■ If displayed time is correct, press **ENTER**, or
      ■ Type current time (e.g., 16:30 or 16:30:45) and press **ENTER**
5. When operating system prompt (e.g., A> or C>) appears, DOS has been fully loaded. You can now type commands or run programs.

Shut Down and Restart Your Computer

At any time, you may reboot your computer (save files first and close open applications). This erases all information in memory. This procedure describes a "warm" boot, which does not require that you turn off the power of your computer. To perform a "cold" boot, turn off your computer and folllow *START UP YOUR COMPUTER* on page 8.

1. To perform a "warm" boot, place boot disk into Drive A:, or, to boot from hard disk, remove all floppy disks and leave drive doors open
2. Simultaneously press **CTRL** **ALT** **DEL**
3. If prompted, respond to date and time prompts

Stop or Step CONFIG.SYS and AUTOEXEC.BAT Files

1. During booting, while "Starting MS-DOS" appears on the screen:
   - If desired, to boot without the computer reading CONFIG.SYS and executing AUTOEXEC.BAT, press **F5** (Stop Startup) or hold down **SHIFT**, or
   - If desired, to accept or reject each CONFIG.SYS command in turn and to run or not run AUTOEXEC.BAT after CONFIG.SYS, press **F8** (Step Startup)

NOTE: For more information, see page 83.

Shut Down Your Computer

You may turn off your computer at any time, as long as your disk drive lights are off. Also, make sure you first save all your work onto a floppy or hard disk; otherwise, files you are creating or editing will be erased from your computer's memory.

1. Save work that is still in the computer's memory. Follow the save procedure specified in the reference manual of the program you are currently using.
2. Exit the program properly, thus returning control to DOS (A> or C>)
3. Make sure disk drive lights are off. Turn off your computer, and, if necessary, turn off the power of the monitor, printer, modem, and other components.
4. Remove any floppy disks and store them in their protective sleeves

TYPING DOS COMMANDS

TYPING AND EDITING

Guidelines

- You perform DOS commands by typing the relevant command verb (e.g., COPY, ERASE) and, on the same line, the files to be affected or created and any other desired parameters or switches. DOS executes the command when you press `ENTER`.
- After the command verb, some commands require *parameters* (further information). When filenames are parameters, you usually type the *source* filename first and then the *destination* filename.

  Example: **COPY A:LETTER1 B:** (copies the file from disk in Drive A: to disk in Drive B:)
- After the command verb, you might add a *switch*. Switches modify the duty of the command. For example, in the DIR command, /W displays files in wide screen format. Switches start with / (slash).
- DOS is not sensitive to upper or lower case. You can type in upper or lower case or mixed cases. (**SALES** = **Sales** = **sales**)

Type a Command

1. Type command. While typing a command, you can use these editing keys:
   - To erase the previous character, press `BACKSPACE`
   - To erase the entire command, press `ESC` and press `ENTER`
2. To execute command, press `ENTER`

Reissue Previous Command

1. To make the last command you typed reappear, press `F3`

Interrupt an Operation (Break)

1. - To interrupt a command, press `CTRL` `BREAK`, or
   - Press `CTRL` `C`

Clear the Screen

1. Type **CLS** and press `ENTER`

View Help

1. - For general help, type **HELP**, or
   - For help on a command, type **HELP** **commandname** or type **commandname** /?
2. Press `ENTER`

USING FILENAMES

Conventions

- A file specification consists of an optional drive specifier followed by a : (colon), a name, and an optional extension.

  Examples:
  MYGRAPH
  REPORT#1.DOC
  B:CASHFLOW.WS

- A drive specifier tells DOS the location of a file.

  Examples:
  A:LETTER.DOC
  B:LETTER.DOC

- The drive specifier can contain a directory path. Separate directory names with a \ (backslash). See **USING DRIVES AND DIRECTORIES** section on page 15.

  Examples:
  C:\DOS\UTIL
  D:\DB\CLIENTS\RETAIL.DBF

- The length of the name can range from 1 to 8 characters.

- The extension (maximum 3 characters), if used, must be preceded by a period. Three specific extensions are reserved by DOS for special use. Only program files can have the extensions .COM or .EXE. Only batch files can have the extension .BAT.

- The file extension identifies the file type or the program in which it was created. For example, .PCX and .TIF files are specific types of graphics files and .TXT is a text file.

- Allowable characters in a directory name, filename, or extension include:
  A–Z 0–9 ! @ # $ % & ( ) – _ { } ' ' /

- Two files in the same directory cannot have the same name. Two files in separate directories, however, can have the same name.

  Examples:
  D:\MEMOS\SAMPLES.DOC
  D:\PROPOSAL\SAMPLES.DOC

Wildcards

- When situations arise where you need to copy, erase, rename, etc., several files, you may often save time by using *wildcard* characters in a filename.
- Wildcards allow you to refer to a group of files all in one command.
- A wildcard character stands for any character(s) in its place:
  - ***** (asterisk) refers to any character or any number of remaining characters in the filename or extension.

    Examples:

    *.BAK (refers to any filename that contains the extension .BAK)
    MYFILE.* (refers to all files named MYFILE with any extension)
    . (refers to all files in the current directory)

  - **?** (question mark) refers to any single character in that position.

    Examples:

    LETTER?.DOC (would refer to both LETTER1.DOC and LETTER2.DOC)
    LETTER.BA? (would refer to both LETTER.BAK and LETTER.BAT)

- Further examples:

  COPY A:*.* B: (copies all files in A: to B:)
  DIR *.DOC (lists files with .DOC extension)
  RENAME B:ART???.* *.OLD (adds .OLD extension to all six-character filenames in B: beginning with ART)

Type: Wildcards

Device Names

- When you are typing a command, DOS allows you to specify device names of hardware components. You might do this for example, to configure the hardware or to send input and output to a particular device.

- To refer to devices, use the following list:

CON:	Console
COM1: (AUX:)	Serial (communication) port
COM2:	Second serial port
COM3:	Third serial port
COM4:	Fourth serial port
LPT1: (PRN:)	First parallel (printer) port
LPT2:	Second parallel port
LPT3:	Third parallel port
NUL:	Empty location
CAS1:	Cassette port

Examples:

COPY CON MEMO2 (creates an ASCII file which you type in from the keyboard)

MODE COM1:1200,N,8,1,P (initializes serial port, sets communication protocol)

USING INTERNAL AND EXTERNAL COMMANDS

Guidelines

- Some DOS commands are *internal* commands while others are *external*.

  - Internal commands are stored in memory while the computer is turned on. Any directory can be current when you issue an internal command. Your computer will look in memory to find that command.

    Examples: **COPY   DIR**

  - External commands are less commonly used commands that reside as .COM or .EXE files on a disk. As with all .COM or .EXE programs, the commands work if: (1) the directory containing the file is current, (2) you specify the drive and directory in your command, or (3) the directory is in the specified PATH (see next point).

    In this guide, procedures that require an external command will contain the step "Insert DOS disk and make that drive current."

You do not need to perform this step if either condition 2 or 3 above is true.

Examples:
C>**CHKDSK B:** (if the CHKDSK.COM file exists in the current directory or is specified in the PATH)
A>**C:\DOS\CHKDSK B:** (if the CHKDSK.COM file is not in the current directory or is not specified in the PATH)

- You can store your DOS files in any directory and be able to issue DOS commands from any other drive or directory with the use of the PATH command. This tells your computer which drives and directories to search for DOS or other program files. See *CREATE DIRECTORY PATH* procedure on page 19.

- Executable (program) files end with .COM, .EXE, or .BAT. In order to run these programs, you type the filename   you do not need to type the extension.

USING DRIVES AND DIRECTORIES

Guidelines

- DOS helps you manage files that are stored on floppy disks and hard disks. When you are issuing a DOS command, however, you must tell your computer which *drive* holds the disk containing the information you would like to manipulate.

- In addition to specifying a drive, you must also specify a *directory* within a drive (if the disk is divided into directories).

- If you do not specify a drive and directory, DOS will assume you are referring to the *current* (open) directory on the *logged* drive. The logged drive is indicated by the DOS prompt (e.g., A>, B>, C>).

- Directories (or subdirectories) are a means of organizing files into logical groups using a tree-like structure.

  - Much like a family tree diagram, a directory containing other directories can be called a *parent* to its subdirectories. Each subdirectory, in turn, can be a parent of further subdirectories.

  - The directory that contains all other directories on the disk is called the *root* directory.

  - Organize your directories into sections containing different software programs and their related data files, or place files of similar subject matter in their own directories.

  - You can create directories on hard disks *and* on floppy disks.

  - You can create a virtually unlimited number of directories and subdirectories on a disk.

  - Pre-2.0 versions of DOS do not recognize or allow the creation of directories.

- You can substitute a drive nickname for a subdirectory. This helps you refer more quickly to the subdirectory or use programs that do not recognize subdirectories. See *SUBSTITUTE A DRIVE NAME FOR A DIRECTORY* procedure on page 20.

Diagram of Subdirectories

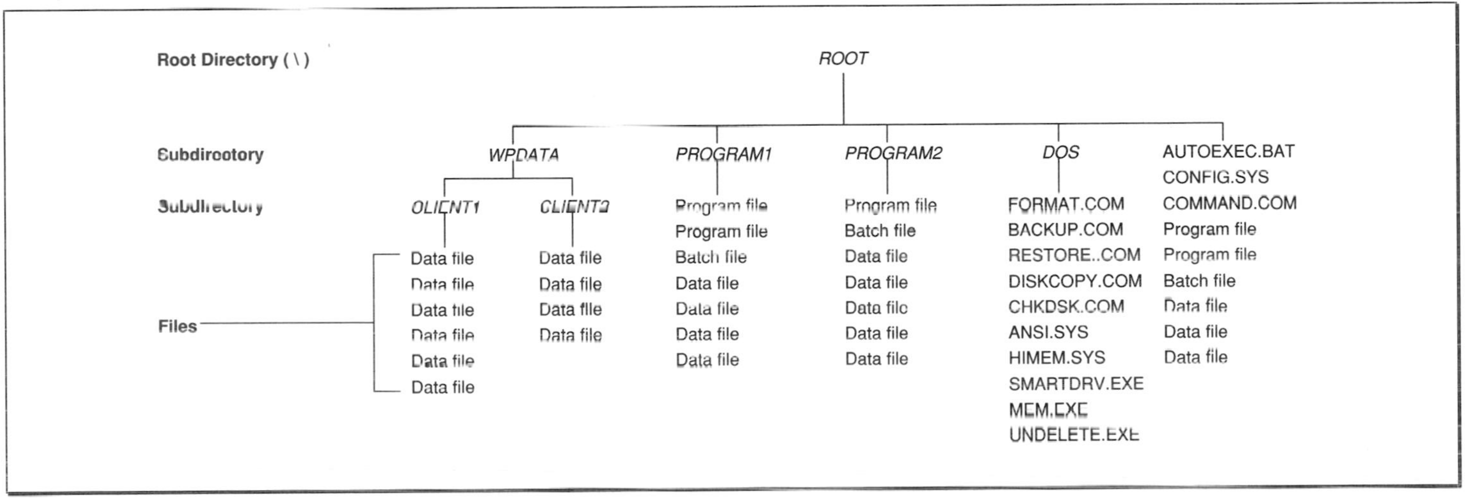

Root Directory (\ )
ROOT
Subdirectory
WPDATA
PROGRAM1
PROGRAM2
DOS
Subdirectory
CLIENT1
CLIENT2
Files
Data file
Data file
Data file
Data file
Data file
Data file
Data file
Data file
Data file
Data file
Program file
Program file
Batch file
Data file
Data file
Data file
Data file
Program file
Batch file
Data file
Data file
Data file
Data file
Data file
FORMAT.COM
BACKUP.COM
RESTORE..COM
DISKCOPY.COM
CHKDSK.COM
ANSI.SYS
HIMEM.SYS
SMARTDRV.EXE
MEM.EXE
UNDELETE.EXE
AUTOEXEC.BAT
CONFIG.SYS
COMMAND.COM
Program file
Program file
Batch file
Data file
Data file
Data file

Change Current Directory

1. ■ To change to root directory, type **CHDIR** \ (or **CD** \) and press
   ENTER
   ■ To change to parent directory, type **CHDIR** .. (or **CD** ..) and
   press **ENTER**
   ■ To change to a subdirectory of the current directory, type
   CHDIR (or **CD**), press **SPACEBAR**, type a list of subdirectories
   to the subdirectory you wish (separate each subsequent
   subdirectory with a \), and press **ENTER**
   Example: **CD BASIC**
   ■ To change to a directory that is not a subdirectory of the current
   directory, type **CHDIR** \ (or **CD** \), type a list of subdirectories
   from the root directory to the subdirectory you wish (separate
   each subsequent subdirectory with a \), and press **ENTER**
   Example: **CD \DOS\BASIC**

NOTE: To change the default directory to a directory on another
drive, first follow *CHANGE LOGGED DRIVE* procedure. To remain in
the same directory, but change the current directory on another drive,
type **CD drive:pathname** (e.g., A>**CD C:**).

View Current Directory

Use this procedure to view the name of the current directory on the
logged drive.

1. ■ To display the current directory of the logged drive, type **CHDIR**
   (or **CD**), or
   ■ To display the current directory on another drive, type **CHDIR**
   (or **CD**) **drive:**
2. Press **ENTER**

Change Logged Drive

1. At the operating system prompt, type the drive letter, (e.g., A, B,
   C), **:** (colon), and press **ENTER**
2. The operating system prompt will display the new logged drive

Example: A>**C:** (switches to the C: drive)

Make a Directory

DOS allows you to create virtually as many directories as you wish on a disk. Remember, however, that when you refer to a directory by its pathname (e.g., \DOS\UTILITY), the pathname can only be 63 characters long, so you may not want to embed directories too deeply in the hierarchical structure.

1. Change directories to the parent directory to contain the new subdirectory
2. Type **MKDIR** (or **MD**) **directoryname**
3. Press `ENTER`

NOTES:
A directory name can be up to 8 characters long and can contain an optional extension. Some computer systems do not allow directory name extensions.

The name and extension cannot be the same name and extension as a file within the parent directory.

Remove a Directory

In order to delete a directory, the directory must be empty of all subdirectories and all files (except for the files named . and ..). To first empty the directory of files, follow *DELETE ALL FILES IN DIRECTORY* procedure on page 31. Also see DELTREE on page 112.

1. Change current directory to the parent of the directory to remove
2. Type **RMDIR** (or **RD**) **directoryname**
3. Press `ENTER`

Examples:
RMDIR SURVEY
RD DRIVERS

Rename a Directory

1. Type **MOVE oldname newname**. You cannot move a directory to a new location (i.e., the directory path of the newname must be the same as that of the oldname).
2. Press `ENTER`

Example:
MOVE C:\WORDPROC C:\WORDS

Create Directory Path

This procedure creates a search PATH in your DOS environment. DOS will search the current directory, then the first pathname in the PATH, then the second pathname, etc., until it finds the .COM, .EXE, or .BAT program file you specify. The program will then be executed. PATH does not search for files with non-program extensions and does not remain in the directory in which it found the program file. (To have an application program search the correct directories for its data files, install the program with instructions on where to search.)

1. Type **PATH full pathname1;full pathname2;other pathnames**
2. Press **ENTER**

Example:
   PATH C:\DOS;C:.;C:\BIN;C:\;..;C:\WP

NOTES:
Be sure to separate each directory with a ; (semicolon).

Specify pathnames from the root directory (e.g., C:\) so that PATH will find the program or batch file no matter what directory is current.

Use the .. symbol to refer to the parent directory. The . (single period) symbol is useful for referring to the current directory of another drive (e.g., **C:.**).

If a directory listed in the PATH command is not a valid directory, DOS will skip it and search the next directory without displaying an error message. If the program or batch file is not found in either the current directory or in a directory specified in PATH, an error message will appear.

To store a search PATH for future use, place the PATH command in a batch file such as AUTOEXEC.BAT.

A PATH statement can be up to 127 characters long, including the PATH command.

View Current Directory Path
1. Type **PATH**
2. Press **ENTER**

Delete Directory Path
The PATH statement is in memory until you either use this procedure to remove it from memory or until you shut down your computer.

1. Type **PATH ;**
2. Press **ENTER**

NOTE: After you delete a PATH statement, you can still change directories to run a program. DOS always searches for a file in the current directory.

Substitute a Drive Name for a Directory
This external command renames a subdirectory as a drive name (e.g., D:, E:) for the current session. This allows you to refer more quickly to a subdirectory or use a program that does not recognize subdirectories

1. Type **SUBST newdrive:pathname**
2. Press **ENTER**

Example: **SUBST E: C:\WS\FILES**

NOTE: To delete a substitution, type **/D** instead of pathname. The substitution is in memory until you either delete it or shut down your computer.

Example: **SUBST E: /D**

USING BATCH FILES

Guidelines

- Batch files are program files (ending with .BAT) that you can create to execute DOS commands for you. To execute the commands, run the batch file. The content of these ASCII files is limited to DOS commands and simple batch file programming commands.

- To have a batch file execute automatically when you start up your computer, name the file AUTOEXEC.BAT and store it in the root directory of your boot disk.

- This simple batch file changes the directory to 123, executes 123, and returns to the root directory when you exit 123:

```
c:
cd \123
123
cd \
```

Create a Batch File

Batch files must be ASCII files (see page 35). Create a batch file using your word processing program in ASCII mode, using EDLIN (see page 94), using EDIT (see page 97), or create it as follows:

1. At the operating system prompt, type **COPY CON newname.BAT** and press `ENTER`
2. Type the desired commands. Type each command on a separate line.
3. To save and exit file:
   - Press `F6` and press `ENTER` , or
   - Press `CTRL` `Z` , then press `ENTER`

NOTE: At any time, to exit without saving the file, press `CTRL` `BREAK` (or press `CTRL` `C`).

Edit a Batch File

1. Use your word processor in ASCII mode, EDLIN, or EDIT to edit a batch file

Display a Batch File

1. Type **TYPE filename.BAT**
2. Press **ENTER**
3. ▪ To pause scrolling at any point, press **CTRL** **NUM LOCK** (or press **CTRL** **S**). To resume scrolling, press any key. Or,
   ▪ To stop scrolling and return to DOS prompt, press **CTRL** **BREAK** (or press **CTRL** **C**)

Run a Batch File

1. Type the batch file name (you do not need to type the .BAT extension). If typing parameters, type a space and type parameters, separating each parameter with a space.
2. Press **ENTER**

NOTES:
If a command in a batch file does not work correctly, DOS displays an error message and moves on to execute the next command in the file. To see error messages when testing a batch file, remove the ECHO OFF statement from the batch file if necessary.

If DOS runs a different program than your batch file, you might have named the batch file the same name as a program file or DOS command. For example, if WP runs the WP.EXE program, you might experience problems running a batch file named WP.BAT.

Interrupt a Batch File

1. At any time, you can interrupt the running of a batch file:
   ▪ To pause temporarily, press **CTRL** **NUM LOCK** (or press **CTRL** **S**). To resume running file, press any key. Or,
   ▪ To stop a batch file and return to DOS prompt, press **CTRL** **BREAK** (or press **CTRL** **C**)

NOTE: You might have to repeat the keystrokes to stop the batch file.

Use Programming Commands

- You can type a maximum of 9 parameters when you issue the batch file command. % markers in the batch file refer to these parameters. When you type the command, separate the parameters with a space.

  Example: **RUNTEST 3 Y**

- Parameter marker %0 within a batch file refers to the filename of the batch file. Markers %1–%9 refer to the subsequent parameters. Use the SHIFT command to accept more than 9 parameters.

- Use programming commands (CHOICE, GOTO, FOR, IF) to create branches, loops, and conditional statements.

- Instruct the user by printing remarks to the screen (ECHO, PAUSE, REM).

- Find batch file subcommands in the **BATCH FILE COMMANDS AND EXAMPLES** section on page 135.

Sample Batch File

```
echo off
rem This file copies all .DOC files.
echo Place data disk in B:
pause
copy a:\*.doc b:
```

Using AUTOEXEC.BAT

- AUTOEXEC.BAT is an important file. It is created automatically when you install DOS on a hard disk. It sets up your DOS environment each time you start up your computer. For example, it tells DOS about components (such as a mouse or extra memory) that are connected to or built into your computer.
- Use AUTOEXEC.BAT to save time by placing in the file certain DOS commands that you use often. For example, if you commonly type a PATH statement to tell DOS where to find program files that you often run, enter the PATH statement in AUTOEXEC.BAT and DOS will always know where to find the program files.
- Add a *startup procedure* to AUTOEXEC.BAT to set the DOS environment each time you start up your computer. For example, a startup procedure could display the current date and time and give you the opportunity to correct it. Then the startup procedure could begin running a word processor, DOSSHELL, or Windows.
- DOS runs AUTOEXEC.BAT each time you turn on your computer. If you change AUTOEXEC.BAT, turn off your computer. Start your computer again, and the AUTOEXEC.BAT file will execute.

- DOS commands commonly found in AUTOEXEC.BAT: @ECHO OFF, PATH, PROMPT, SET COMSPEC, VERIFY OFF, SET DIRCMD, DOSKEY, DOSSHELL, SMARTDRV, UNDELETE.
- Remember that DOS also executes the commands in another file named CONFIG.SYS when you start up your computer (see **USING CONFIG.SYS** on page 80).

Create an AUTOEXEC.BAT File

Most boot disks already have an AUTOEXEC.BAT file. First, use the **DIR** command to see if one exists. If it does, follow *EDIT A BATCH FILE* or *DISPLAY A BATCH FILE* procedures on pages 21–22. If an AUTOEXEC.BAT file does *not* exist, follow this procedure.

1. ▪ If booting from a floppy disk, insert boot disk in logged drive, or
   ▪ If booting from a hard disk, make root directory of hard disk current (e.g., **CD **)
2. Type **COPY CON AUTOEXEC.BAT** and press `ENTER`
3. Type desired commands, each command on a separate line
4. To save and exit file:
   ▪ Press `F6` and press `ENTER`, or
   ▪ Press `CTRL` `Z`, then press `ENTER`

FILE MANAGEMENT PROCEDURES

LISTING DIRECTORIES

Some of these procedures use the | character (found on the \ key) to pipe information from one program into another. For a complete explanation of piping, see **REDIRECTING AND PIPING INFORMATION** section on page 92.

List Filenames
Use this procedure to view filenames and directory names, file sizes, and modification dates.

1. ■ To view all filenames in directory, type **DIR**, or
   ■ To view information on a single file, type **DIR filename**, or
   ■ To view filenames that match wildcard criteria, type **DIR criteria**, or
   ■ To view all filenames in a different directory, type **DIR pathname**, or
   ■ To view all filenames on another drive, type **DIR drive:**
2. Press **ENTER**

Examples:
   DIR B:
   DIR *.DOC
   DIR N*.*

List All Directory Names on a Disk
1. Insert DOS disk and make that drive current
2. Type **TREE drive:**
3. Press **ENTER**

Examples: **TREE C:**
   TREE A: /F (list filenames)

Pause Scrolling of Display
At any time while the DIR or TREE commands are displaying information on the screen, to temporarily stop the scrolling:

1. Press **CTRL** **NUM LOCK** (or press **CTRL** **S**)
2. To resume scrolling, press any key

Quit Scrolling of Display
To interrupt a DIR or TREE command and return to DOS prompt:

1. Press **CTRL** **BREAK** (or press **CTRL** **C**)

List Filenames by Page

1. Type **DIR** /P
2. Press ENTER
3. When the screen is full, the display will pause until you press a key

Examples:
DIR /P
DIR B:*.TXT /P

List Filenames in Wide Screen Format

Use this procedure to view up to five columns of filenames and directory names on the screen at one time.

1. Type **DIR** /W
2. Press ENTER

Examples:
DIR /W
DIR A: /W

Shortcut with DIR Command

With the DIR command, you do not need to type an * wildcard to represent (1) a filename, or (2) a period and extension.

Examples:
DIR .FMT (lists all files with .FMT extension)
DIR CUST (lists all CUST files with extensions, e.g., CUST.135)
DIR MYCHART. (lists the file named MYCHART)
DIR *. (lists all files and directories in root without extensions)

List Files in Subdirectories
1. Type **DIR** **/S**
2. Press **ENTER**

List Files Alphabetically
You can also sort listing by group (directories first), extension, and date.

1. To sort by name, type **DIR** **/O**
2. Press **ENTER**

Examples:
   DIR **/OG** (directories first)
   DIR **/OE** (by extension)
   DIR **/OD** (by date)
   DIR **/P** **/OGEN** **/A** (combination of switches)
   DIR B: **|** **SORT** (by name)
   DIR **|** **SORT** **/+10** (by extension)
   DIR **|** **SORT** **/+13** (by size)

/0N = alph by name

Preset DIR Switches
1. In AUTOEXEC.BAT file or at DOS prompt, type
   SET **DIRCMD=/x** **/x** **/x...**
2. Press **ENTER**

Example: **SET DIRCMD=/P** **/OGEN** **/A**

/A: attributes
*   H = hidden files*
* −H = not " "*
*   S = system "*
* −S = not " "*
*   D = directories / −D*
* A/−A = files ready for archiving*
* R/−R = Read-only files*

PRINTING AND STORING DIRECTORIES

Guidelines

- Some of these procedures use the < or > characters, which redirect standard input and standard output. For a complete explanation of redirecting standard input and standard output, see **REDIRECTING AND PIPING INFORMATION** section on page 92.

- Some of these procedures use the | character (found on the \ key) to pipe information from one program into another. For a complete explanation of piping, see **REDIRECTING AND PIPING INFORMATION** section on page 92.

- PRN refers to LPT1:. If your printer is connected to a different parallel port, substitute LPT2: or LPT3: for PRN.

Print Filenames

1. Type **DIR > PRN**
2. Press **ENTER**

Print Directory Names

1. Insert DOS disk and make that drive current
2. Type **TREE drive: > PRN**
3. Press **ENTER**

Print Directory Names and Filenames

1. Insert DOS disk and make that drive current
2. Type **TREE drive: /F > PRN**
3. Press **ENTER**

NOTE: To use ASCII characters (+ – | \) instead of extended characters, add the /A switch after /F.

Send Filenames to a File

1. Type **DIR > filename**
2. Press **ENTER**
3. If desired, **TYPE** file to the screen or view file in your word processor

Examples:

DIR > MYFILES
DIR A:*.TXT > B:TEXTFILE.DIR
DIR /B > LIST.1 (omits summary, size, and date)

Send Directory Names and Filenames to a File

1. Insert DOS disk and make that drive current
2. Type **TREE drive: /F > filename**
3. Press **ENTER**
4. If desired, **TYPE** file to the screen or view file in your word processor

Example:

TREE C: /F > A:ALLFILES.1
DIR C: /S > FILES

RENAMING, DELETING, COPYING, AND MOVING FILES

Use the following procedures to clean out unneeded files, copy files, and rename files.

Rename a File
1. Make directory containing file current
2. Type **RENAME** (or **REN**) **oldname newname**
3. Press **ENTER**

Example: **REN MONTH.RPT JAN.RPT**

Rename a Group of Files
To review wildcards, see *WILDCARDS* on page 12.

1. Make directory containing files current
2. Type **RENAME** (or **REN**) **oldcriteria newcriteria**
3. Press **ENTER**

Examples:
RENAME B:*.XTR *.ALL (changes .XTR extension to .ALL)
REN HOME*.* *.PVT (changes extension of HOME files to .PVT)

NOTE: RENAME command will stop if a name that you want to change to already exists.

Delete a File

This procedure permanently deletes the indicated file from the directory you specify. If necessary, first back up the file by copying it to another disk or directory.

1. Make directory containing file current
2. Type **ERASE** (or **DEL**) **filename**
3. Press **ENTER**

NOTE: Include the file extension as part of the filename.

Examples:
  ERASE REPORT.TXT
  DEL JUNK1.DOC

Delete a Group of Files

This procedure permanently deletes files from the directory you specify. If necessary, first back up the files by copying them.

NOTE: Be careful when using wildcards to erase files. To review the use of wildcards, see *WILDCARDS* on page 12. Use a drive specifier to be certain that you are erasing files from the correct drive.

1. Make directory containing files current
2. Type **ERASE** (or **DEL**) **criteria**
3. Press **ENTER**

Example: **DEL A:*.BAK**

Delete All Files in Directory

This procedure permanently deletes all files on the disk or directory you specify. If necessary, first back up the files. Also see the DELTREE command on page 112.

1. Make directory containing files current
2. Type **ERASE** (or **DEL**) **drive:\path*.*** (Use drive and full pathname to avoid errors.)
3. Press **ENTER**
4. To verify command, type **Y**
5. Press **ENTER**

Example: **DEL B:*.*** (erases all files on B:)

NOTE: You can erase all files in a directory by typing **ERASE** (or **DEL**) **directoryname**. This will not remove the directory—only the files contained in it.

Example: **DEL \WPDATA** (erases all files in WPDATA subdirectory)

Undelete File(s)

You have more options in undeleting files if you load Undelete into memory before you delete files. There are three types of undelete protection. Delete Sentry gives you maximum protection but requires a small amount of disk space and memory. Delete Tracker provides slightly less protection and requires some memory. If you do not use either of these two methods to set up undeletion, you might still be able to undelete erased files if they have not been overwritten on disk. You can set up undeletion by adding any of the commands listed at right to your AUTOEXEC.BAT file or typing them at the DOS prompt.

When you installed DOS 6.0 on your computer, you had the option of installing Undelete for Windows and MS-DOS, Windows only, MS-DOS only, or None. To use the Undelete program in DOS, you had to install it for Windows and MS-DOS or for MS-DOS only.

1. ▪ To list files you can undelete, type **UNDELETE path /LIST**, or
   ▪ To undelete a file, type **UNDELETE filename**, or
   ▪ To undelete a group of files, type **UNDELETE criteria**
2. Press **ENTER**

Examples:
   UNDELETE *.BAK
   UNDELETE (restores all deleted files DOS can locate on the disk)

Undelete Options

UNDELETE /LOAD	(loads memory-resident portion of Delete Sentry or Delete Tracker into memory using information in UNDELETE.INI file, if present; otherwise, uses default settings)
UNDELETE /SC	(loads Delete Sentry program into memory using UNDELETE.INI settings, if present, and enables protection of Drive C: or, if UNDELETE.INI specifies drives, protects those drives, rather than the drive specified after /S)
UNDELETE /TC–300	(loads Delete Tracker program into memory, creates PCTRACKER.DEL file to track up to 300 files, and enables tracking for Drive C:)
UNDELETE /U	(unloads memory-resident portion of Undelete command from memory, disables command)
UNDELETE /STATUS	(displays protection in effect on each drive)

Copy a File to Another Disk

The copied file overwrites any file in the destination directory that contains the same filename as the copied file.

1. Make the target directory in the destination disk current
2. Make directory containing file current
3. Type **COPY filename drive:**
4. Press ENTER

Example: **COPY FRANK.DOC C:**

Copy a File to Another Directory

1. Make directory containing file current
2. Type **COPY filename pathname**
3. Press ENTER

NOTE: Specify the destination directory in the "pathname."

Examples:

  COPY FRANK.DOC .. (copies FRANK.DOC to parent directory)
  COPY FRANK.DOC \REPORTS\APR (If APR is not a valid directory name under REPORTS, FRANK.DOC will be stored in a file called APR.)

Copy a File and Rename It

This procedure is useful for copying a file to the same directory, since two files in the same directory cannot have the same name.

1. Make directory containing file current
2. Type **COPY filename newname**
3. Press ENTER

Example: **COPY NOV11.DOC NOV11A.DOC**

Copy a File into Current Directory

1. Make directory to contain file current
2. Type **COPY filename**
3. Press ENTER

Example: B>**COPY A:PATIENTS.REF** (copies from A: to B:)

Copy a Large File to Another Hard Disk

Use this procedure to transfer a file that is larger than a floppy disk.

1. ▪ Link two computers together with a cable and follow *LINK TWO COMPUTERS* procedure on page 69, or
   ▪ Back up and restore file with floppy disks using procedures in **BACKING UP A HARD DISK** section on page 61

Copy a Group of Files

To review wildcards, see *WILDCARDS* on page 12.

1. Make directory containing files current
2. Type **COPY criteria destination**
3. Press **ENTER**

Examples:
> **COPY *.SET C:**
> **COPY *.SET *.OLD** (this gives the copies an .OLD extension)
> **COPY *.SET \DOS\DRIVERS**

Copy All Files in Directory

1. Make directory containing files current
2. Type **COPY *.* destination**
3. Press **ENTER**

Example: **COPY *.* B:**

Move a File

The moved file overwrites any file in the destination directory that contains the same filename as the moved file.

1. Insert DOS disk and make that drive current
2. Type **MOVE filename destination** (a destination is required)
3. Press **ENTER**

Examples:
> **MOVE A:SPRING93.DOC B:**
> **MOVE C:\DATA\BUDGET.WK1 C:\YEARLY**
> **MOVE C:\WORDS\RECIPE.WP .** (period indicates the current directory)

Move a Group of Files

1. Insert DOS disk and make that drive current
2. Type **MOVE criteria destination** (a destination is required)
3. Press **ENTER**

Examples:
> **MOVE A:*.* B:**
> **MOVE C:\WORDS\REPORT*.* C:\WORDS\PROJECT**

Move Files

MANAGING ASCII FILES

Guidelines

- ASCII files contain only standard letters, numbers, or symbols and certain control characters. ASCII files are stored in simple line-by-line format.

- A **CTRL Z** (^Z) marks the end of an ASCII file.

- Use the following procedures to sort the contents of a file, find a text string within files, and concatenate files.

- Use *concatenation* to append one file to the end of another existing file or to combine several files. You can concatenate ASCII files or non-ASCII files (binary files such as program files or non-ASCII data files). However, DOS treats each file as an ASCII file and will only transfer up to the first end-of-file (^Z) marker and ignore the rest of the file.

Create an ASCII File

Use this procedure to quickly create an unformatted, standard-character file. This is useful for creating a batch file.

1. Type **COPY CON newname**

2. Press **ENTER**

3. Type contents of file line by line. End each line by pressing **ENTER** .

4. To save and exit file:
   - Press **F6** and press **ENTER** , or
   - Press **CTRL Z** , then press **ENTER**

NOTE: At any time, to exit without saving file, press **CTRL BREAK** (or press **CTRL C**).

Display ASCII File

Use this procedure to view the contents of an ASCII file on your screen. This is useful for viewing batch files.

1. - If displaying a short file, type **TYPE filename**, or
   - If displaying a long file, type **TYPE filename | MORE**

2. Press **ENTER**

3. - To pause scrolling at any point, press **CTRL NUM LOCK** (or press **CTRL S**). To resume scrolling, press any key. Or,
   - To stop scrolling and return to DOS prompt, press **CTRL BREAK** (or press **CTRL C**)

Sort a File

Use this procedure to arrange the lines in a file in numerical and alphabetical order or in reverse numerical and alphabetical order. You can either replace the file or create a new file.

1. Insert DOS disk and make that drive current
2. ■ To sort in numerical and alphabetical order, type
   SORT < file to sort > destination, or
   ■ To sort in reverse numerical and alphabetical order, type
   SORT /R < file to sort > destination
3. Press **ENTER**

Examples:
   SORT < B:GRADES > B:GRADES
   SORT < \LIST\MEMBERS > \LIST\MEMBERS.NEW
   SORT /R < B:EARNINGS.92 > B:EARNINGS.92R

Sort a File Based on Specified Column

Use this procedure to sort a file in numerical and alphabetical or in reverse order based on an offset of a specified number of characters. You can either replace the file or create a new file.

1. Insert DOS disk and make that drive current

2. ■ To sort in numerical and alphabetical order, type
   SORT /+number < file to sort > destination, or
   ■ To sort in reverse numerical and alphabetical order, type
   SORT /R /+number < file to sort > destination
3. Press **ENTER**

Examples:
   SORT /+9 < B:MYFILES > B:MYFILES
   SORT /R /+24 < EXPENSES.LST > HIGHEST.EXP

Sort a File on the Screen

You can view a sorted version of a file without changing the file itself.

1. Insert DOS disk and make that drive current
2. Use one of the following options:
   ■ To sort, type **SORT < filename**, or
   ■ To sort in reverse order, type **SORT /R < filename**, or
   ■ To sort by column, type **SORT /+number < filename**, or
   ■ To sort in reverse order by column, type **SORT /R /+number < filename**
3. Press **ENTER**

Example: **SORT < DATE1ST**

Find a Text String within File(s)

Use this procedure to display the lines, line numbers, and/or line count of files that contain a specified text string.

1. Insert DOS disk and make that drive current
2. Use one of the following options:
   - To display all lines that contain string, type **FIND "string" file list**, or
   - To display all lines that do not contain string, type **FIND /V "string" file list**, or
   - To count all the occurrences per file of lines that contain string, type **FIND /C "string" file list**, or
   - To display all line numbers and lines that contain string, type **FIND /N "string" file list**, or
   - Combine switches /**V** and /**N**
3. Press **ENTER**

Examples:

FIND "708" PHONE.LST (displays all lines containing 708)

FIND /V "MR." A:ADDRESS (displays all lines that do not contain MR.)

FIND /C "American" \LETTERS (counts all lines that contain American)

FIND /N "18584" ACCTS (displays line numbers and lines containing 18584)

FIND /V /N "California" 92SAL 93SAL (displays line numbers and lines not containing California)

Concatenate ASCII Files

Join as many files as desired. You can join non-ASCII (or binary) files using this method, but DOS will only transfer up to the first end-of-file (^Z) marker and ignore the rest of the file.

1. Type **COPY file1 + file2 + (other names) newname**
2. Press **ENTER**

NOTE: File1 will be moved to the new file, file2 will append to the new file after file1, etc.

Example:
COPY CAL.LST + ORE.LST + WASH.LST WEST.ALL (You can also use wildcard criteria to perform this: **COPY *.LST WEST.ALL**.)

Append ASCII File(s) onto Existing File

Use this command to append specified files onto "file1." You can join non-ASCII (or binary) files using this method, but DOS will only transfer up to the first end-of-file (^Z) marker and ignore the rest of the file.

1. Type **COPY file1 + file2 + (other names)**
2. Press **ENTER**

Example:
COPY CLASSA + CLASSB + CLASSC + CLASSD (combines all files into CLASSA)

PRINTING

Guidelines

- Although you may perform most printing tasks using applications software, it is useful to know how to perform DOS printing procedures.

- DOS allows you to send a snapshot of the screen directly to the printer, to send all output to the printer thus recording a DOS session, and to print an ASCII file directly from DOS. The PRINT command, however, has no text formatting capability and only prints ASCII files.

- You can issue the command to PRINT a file and then perform another task while DOS is printing in the background. If you issue several PRINT commands, the print jobs are stored in a *queue*. You can view the files in the queue, remove a file, or cancel the entire queue.

- The first time you use the PRINT command, you will be asked for an output device. Press **ENTER** for the default of PRN (LPT1), or type a specific device name (e.g., **LPT2, COM1**) and press **ENTER** .

- With the MODE command, you can elect to send printing to the serial port.

Set Default Printer

The first time you print, DOS asks you for the output device. You can use this procedure to specify a printer at any time.

1. Type **PRINT /D:device**
2. Press **ENTER**

Examples
  PRINT /D:LPT1
  PRINT /D:COM1

Set Printer On/Off

Use this procedure to send information to the printer as it is being displayed on the screen. This is helpful in printing directories of files, printing ASCII files as you TYPE them to the screen, or in "capturing" data transmitted to your terminal.

1. To set printer on, press **CTRL** **PRT SC** (or press **CTRL** **P**)
2. To set printer off, repeat Step 1

NOTE: At any time, to cancel the printing, press **CTRL** **BREAK** (or press **CTRL** **C**).

Print Image Displayed on Screen

1. At any time while in DOS or in many application programs, to send an image of the screen to the printer (characters only, no graphics), press **SHIFT** **PRT SC** (on some keyboards, press **PRINTSCREEN** (without **SHIFT**))

NOTE: You can also use this procedure to quickly check if your printer is connected and your port is properly configured.

Redirect Output to Printer

Use this procedure to send the output of DOS commands to the printer.

1. Type **desired command > PRN**
2. Press **ENTER**

Examples:
   DIR > PRN
   CHKDSK A: > PRN

Print a File

Use this procedure to print an ASCII-formatted file. If you are using a pre-3.0 version of DOS, you can only PRINT a file in the current directory of the logged drive. After issuing the command, you can change directories while the file(s) are still printing.

1. Insert DOS disk and make that drive current
2. Type **PRINT filename**
3. Press **ENTER**

NOTES:
If the file(s) to be printed are not located in the directory containing PRINT.COM, create a directory PATH to PRINT.COM. You can then PRINT from any directory.

Another way to print an ASCII file is to type **COPY filename PRN**. You cannot, however, perform other DOS tasks while printing with this method.

Print a Group of Files

You can have as many as 10 files in the print queue at one time. If you are using a pre-3.0 version of DOS, you can only PRINT files that are in the current directory of the logged drive. After issuing the command, you can change directories while file(s) are still printing.

1. Insert DOS disk and make that drive current
2. ▪ If using wildcard criteria, type **PRINT criteria**, or
   ▪ If listing files, type **PRINT filename1 filename2 (other names)**
3. Press **ENTER**

Examples:
   PRINT *.C
   PRINT JAN.DAT FEB.DAT TOTAL.93

Print a Binary File

1. Type **COPY filename /B printer**
2. Press **ENTER**

Examples:
   COPY SHEET3.PRN /B LPT2
   COPY D:\TOTALS\JAN.DAT /B PRN

View Print Queue
1. Type **PRINT**
2. Press ENTER

NOTES:
The first file in the print queue is the file that is currently being printed.

Files printed with the COPY command do not go to the print queue; they are sent directly to the printer.

Remove a File from Print Queue
1. Type **PRINT filename /C**
2. Press ENTER

Remove All Files from Print Queue
1. Type **PRINT /T**
2. Press ENTER

Set Parallel Port

(DEFAULT = 80 characters/line, 6 lines/inch)

In some cases, you can use this procedure to print in condensed type or change vertical spacing of lines (for IBM Graphics, Epson®, or compatible dot matrix printers). Some application programs reinitialize the printer before printing, which invalidates this setting.

1. Type **MODE LPTnumber:chars,spacing,P**
2. Press **ENTER**

NOTE: *LPTnumber:* can be LPT1:, LPT2:, or LPT3:. *Chars* equals the number of characters per line (80 or 132). DOS uses the word wrapping, hard returns, and line feeds of the file to be printed. *Spacing* equals the vertical lines per inch (6 or 8). The *P* parameter continuously retries to send output to the printer.

Example: **MODE LPT1:132,8,P** (configures port 1)

Set Serial Port

(DEFAULT = Parity E, Databits 7, Stopbits 1)

Use this procedure to initialize a serial port, set communication protocol, or print with a serial printer.

1. Type **MODE COMnumber:baud,parity,databits,stopbits,P**
2. Press **ENTER**

NOTE: *COMnumber:* can be COM1: or COM2: (or COM3: or COM4: on some versions). *Baud* equals the first two digits of the baud rate, e.g., 30=300, 96=9600. *Parity* can be **n** (none), **o** (odd), or **e** (even). *Databits* equals 7 or 8. *Stopbits* equals 1 or 2. The *P* parameter continuously retries to send the output (use for printing).

Examples:
   MODE COM1:12,N,8,1,P
   MODE COM2:3,,,,P

Send Printing to Serial Port Printer

1. Set up serial port (follow *SET SERIAL PORT* procedure)
2. Type **MODE LPTnumber:=COM1:** (or **COM2:**)
3. Press **ENTER**

Example: **MODE LPT1:=COM1:**

NOTE: To disable this redirection, type **MODE LPT1**.

DISK MANAGEMENT PROCEDURES

Guidelines

- DOS enables you to use various types of disk drives. The two major drive types are the floppy disk drive and hard disk drive.
- 5¼-inch floppy disk drives can be single-sided, double-sided, or high-capacity. Single-sided or double-sided disks can be either single-density or double-density (DD).
- Since there are various floppy disk drive types, make sure you use the correct format of floppy disk in a given disk drive (see table at right). DOS cannot read or write to floppy disks with the wrong format for the disk drive.
- The table at right shows standard disk capacities for different drives in kilobytes and megabytes. See the next page for a table defining kilobytes and megabytes.
- Do *not* use high-capacity formatted disks with early DOS versions (pre-3.0) which do not support high-capacity disks. DOS will be unable to read from or write to the disk.

Disk Drive Types

5¼ INCH DRIVE	ALLOWABLE DISKS
Single-sided	Single-sided (160/180K)
Double-sided	Single-sided (160/180K)
	Double-sided (320/360K)
High-capacity	Single-sided (160/180K)
	Double-sided (320/360K)
	High-capacity (1.2M)

3½ INCH DRIVE	ALLOWABLE DISKS
Double-sided	Double-sided (720K)
High-capacity	Double-sided (720K)
	High-capacity (1.44M)

Disk Capacity

- Disk capacity, the amount of information that can be stored on a disk, is measured in *bytes*.
- The first table on this page shows a comparison table of bytes, kilobytes, and megabytes.
- The second table on this page helps you find exact disk sizes.
- Note, however, that a formatted disk has less available space than an unformatted disk. For example, once formatted, a 368,640 byte 5¼-inch floppy disk only has space for 362,496 bytes.

Units of Measure

1 Byte (8 Bits)	=	1 Character
1 Sector	=	512 Bytes
1 K Bytes (Kilobyte)	=	1,024 Bytes
1 M Bytes (Megabyte)	=	1,048,576 Bytes

Common-Sized Disks (in Bytes)

5¼ Inch Disk*	=	362,496 Bytes
5¼ Inch High-Capacity Disk**	=	1,213,952 Bytes
3½ Inch Disk**	=	730,112 Bytes
3½ Inch High-Capacity Disk**	=	1,457,664 Bytes
10 MB Hard Disk	=	approx. 10,000,000 Bytes
20 MB Hard Disk	=	approx. 21,000,000 Bytes
30 MB Hard Disk	=	approx. 31,000,000 Bytes

*Formatted, double-sided, double-density, 9 sectors, 40 tracks.
**Formatted

MANAGING FLOPPY DISKS

Guidelines

- Any one of the following can damage floppy disks or lose data:

Bending	Proximity to:
Touching magnetic surface	Magnetic fields
Extreme temperatures	Radios
Liquids	TVs
Dust or smoke	Speakers

- Because floppy disks can be damaged, it is important to back up your work. For all important programs and data files, make a second copy and store it in a separate location.

- Two procedures can back up floppy disks:

  - Use COPY *.* to add all files (except hidden files, read-only files, and directories) from the source disk to the files that already exist on a formatted target disk. DOS will take files that have become fragmented (stored in different disk locations) and recompose them into contiguous files. Also, DOS copies the files onto undamaged areas of the disk.

  - Use DISKCOPY to automatically erase the target disk and copy all directories and files (including boot, hidden, and read-only files) sector by sector onto the target disk, reformatting the target disk, if necessary. This may cause DOS to write a file onto a damaged sector of the target disk. To prevent this from occurring, first FORMAT the target disk. DOS will check for damaged sectors and report them to you. You may then decide to use a different target disk.

- To further protect information on a disk, if you intend to only read from the disk and not write information to the disk, place tape over the square notch by the label of a disk. This prevents DOS from writing new information to the disk or erasing files from the disk.

- If files have been damaged and you do not have a backup, follow *RECOVER DAMAGED FILE* procedure on page 51 to recover as much of the file as possible. To recover all files on a disk if the disk's directory has been damaged, follow *RECOVER DAMAGED DISK* procedure on page 51

- **For single floppy drive systems:** To refer to a second drive, give it the drive specifier B:. DOS will temporarily reassign Drive A: as Drive B: and prompt you to replace the disk in Drive A:.

Disk: Protect

Copy All Files on a Floppy Disk (COPY *.*)

Use this procedure to copy all files (except hidden files, read-only files, and directories) from one disk to another. The files are copied onto the target disk—this does not erase the files on the target disk. However, any file with the same name and extension is overwritten by the source file.

1. If necessary, place disk to copy in source drive
2. ▪ If using a dual floppy drive system and copying to a disk with no directories, place *target* disk in desired drive, or
   ▪ If copying to a directory, make target directory current
3. Type **COPY drive:*.* target drive:**
4. Press **ENTER**
5. If using a single floppy drive system, follow prompts to replace disks

Example: **COPY A:*.* B:** (Copies all files on A: to B:. Useful for either dual or single floppy drive systems. If using a single floppy disk system, DOS will temporarily reassign disk drive A: as B: when it asks you to insert target disk.)

NOTES:
To also copy subdirectories, use XCOPY (see page 131).

The disk must have enough available space to store the copied files. If it becomes filled with files during the copy process, some files may not be copied onto the target disk. If you are copying a large number of files, follow *CHECK FLOPPY DISK AND MEMORY STATUS* procedure on page 52 first to view available space on the target disk.

Copy Entire Floppy Disk (DISKCOPY)

Use this procedure to copy all files and directories from one floppy disk to another compatible floppy disk. This procedure erases all files on the target disk and formats the disk exactly like the source disk.

NOTE: To protect yourself from making an error in specifying drives, place a write-protect tab on your source disk. To make sure there are no bad sectors on the target disk, first FORMAT the target disk with the *FORMAT A FLOPPY DISK* procedure on pages 49-50.

1. Insert DOS disk and make that drive current
2. Type **DISKCOPY source disk: target drive:**
3. Press **ENTER**
4. When prompted, insert disk(s) (you may now replace the DOS disk) and press any key to begin
5. If using a single floppy drive system or copying disks in the same drive, follow prompts to replace disks
6. When copy is completed, to copy another disk, type **Y**; otherwise, type **N**

Examples:
   Dual drive system: **DISKCOPY A: B:**
   Single drive system: **DISKCOPY A: A:**
   Copy a disk in the current drive: **DISKCOPY**

NOTE: If you have specified a wrong drive, to interrupt the procedure, press **CTRL** **BREAK** (or press **CTRL** **C**). You can also open the drive door to cancel the operation, but if DOS is writing to the disk (drive light is on) when you open the door, the floppy disk could be irreparably damaged.

Format a Floppy Disk (DOS 5–6)

Use this command to prepare a floppy disk to contain files created in DOS. You can format a new or used disk. This procedure erases all files on a disk, reformats the disk, and checks for damaged sectors.

1. Insert DOS disk (may be a hard disk) and make that drive current
2. Type **FORMAT drive:** (see examples)
3. ▪ If disk to format is the same capacity as the disk drive, press **ENTER** , or
   ▪ If the disk has a smaller capacity than the default for that drive, type **/F:x** (see table) and press **ENTER**

Examples:
   FORMAT A: (formats disk in A:)
   FORMAT B: /F:720 (formats disk in B:)

NOTE: To turn the disk into a boot disk (from which you can start up your computer), see **CREATING BOOT DISKS** on page 72.

Unformat a Floppy Disk (DOS 5–6)

Use this DOS 5.0 and 6.0 command to undelete files and directories erased in the FORMAT command.

1. Insert DOS disk (may be a hard disk) and make that drive current
2. ▪ To test if unformat can restore disk, type **UNFORMAT drive: /TEST**, or
   ▪ To unformat disk, type **UNFORMAT drive:**, or
   ▪ To list files and directories found by UNFORMAT command while it is unformatting, type **UNFORMAT drive: /L**
3. Press **ENTER**

/F Switch Options (DOS 5–6)

/F:160 or 160k, 160kb
/F:180 or 180k, 180kb
/F:320 or 320k, 320kb
/F:360 or 360k, 360kb
/F:720 or 720k, 720kb
/F:1.2 or 1200, 1200k, 1200kb, 1.2m, 1.2mb
/F:1.44 or 1440, 1440k, 1440kb, 1.44m. 1.44mb
/F:2.88 or 2880, 2880k, 2880kb, 2.88m, 2.88mb

Format a Floppy Disk (DOS 2–4)

Use this procedure to prepare a floppy disk to contain files created in DOS. You can format a new or used disk. This procedure erases all files on a disk, reformats the disk, and checks for damaged sectors.

NOTE: Avoid inadvertently formatting hard drives C: or D:! Make sure your drive specifier is correct.

1. Insert DOS disk (may be a hard disk) and make that drive current
2. Type **FORMAT drive:** (See examples below.)
3. If desired, to add operating system files to disk (thus making it bootable), press `SPACEBAR` and type **/S**
4. If desired, to label the disk, press `SPACEBAR` and type **/V**
5. If desired, to format a double-sided (360K) disk in a high-capacity drive, press `SPACEBAR` and type **/4**. (This will not make the disk into a high-capacity disk.)
6. If desired, to format a 720K 3½ inch disk in a 1.44M drive, press `SPACEBAR` and type **/N:9 /T:80** (This will not make the disk into a high-capacity disk.)
7. Press `ENTER`
8. When prompted, check that your disks are in the proper drives and press `ENTER`

9. If using a single floppy drive system, follow prompts to replace disks
10. If prompted for a label, if desired, type a name describing the disk (up to 11 characters), then press `ENTER`
11. • To format another disk, type **Y** and follow prompts, or
    • To complete formatting, type **N**

Examples:
   A>**FORMAT B:** (formats disk in B:)
   C>**FORMAT A:** (formats disk in A:)

NOTE: To interrupt formatting before formatting begins, press `CTRL` `BREAK` (or press `CTRL` `C`). To interrupt formatting once formatting has begun, open both drive doors immediately (if DOS is writing to the disk, the disk can be damaged), or press `CTRL` `ALT` `DEL` .

Format: Floppy Disk (DOS 2-4)

Recover Damaged Disk

Use this procedure when a disk's directory has been damaged and you are unable to use files on the disk. This procedure renames all files and directories on the disk to a **FILEnnnn.REC** format and restores the disk directory. You will have to manually rename each file and directory to its original name.

NOTE: Perform this procedure only if the entire disk is unreadable. If only one file or a group of files is damaged, follow *RECOVER A DAMAGED FILE* procedure.

1. Insert DOS disk and make that drive current
2. Type **RECOVER drive:**
3. Press **ENTER**
4. When recovery is complete, rename each file and directory to its original name

Recover a Damaged File

If you receive a DOS disk error message when reading a file, use this procedure to attempt to remove damaged sectors from the file. Each sector equals 512 bytes. This procedure will help you save parts of an ASCII data file, but most likely will not make a .COM or .EXE program file usable.

1. Insert DOS disk and make that drive current
2. Type **RECOVER filename**
3. Press **ENTER**

Check Floppy Disk and Memory Status

Use this procedure to view the label and creation date of a disk, the size of the disk, and the amount of free space on the disk. You will also view the current amount of memory available in your computer.

1. Insert DOS disk and make that drive current
2. Type **CHKDSK drive:**
3. If desired, to have CHKDSK fix the directory or File Allocation Table and allow conversion of lost chains to files, press **SPACEBAR** and type **/F**
4. If desired, to also display all the directories and files on the disk, press **SPACEBAR** and type **/V**
5. Press **ENTER**
6. If using a single floppy drive system, follow prompts to replace disks
7. If prompted to "Convert lost chains to files:"
   - If you typed /F in Step 3, you can create new files that contain the lost clusters. Type **Y** and press **ENTER**. Or,
   - To continue without creating new files, type **N** and press **ENTER**

NOTE: If you respond **Y** to Step 7, you will be able to view the lost

clusters of ASCII files with your word processor or TYPE the files to the screen. The lost cluster files are named FILEnnnn.CHK. If the information is no longer useful to you, erase the lost cluster files and thus free more disk space.

Results of CHKDSK Command

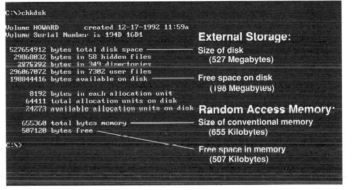

C:\>chkdsk

Volume HOWARD   created 12-17-1992 11:59a
Volume Serial Number is 194D 10D1

527654912 bytes total disk space ——— **External Storage:**
29868032 bytes in 58 hidden files   **Size of disk**
2076292 bytes in 349 directories   **(527 Megabytes)**
296067072 bytes in 7302 user files
198844416 bytes available on disk ——— **Free space on disk**
                                        (198 Megabytes)
8192 bytes in each allocation unit
64411 total allocation units on disk
24273 available allocation units on disk **Random Access Memory:**

655360 total bytes memory ——— **Size of conventional memory**
507120 bytes free ———   **(655 Kilobytes)**

C:\>   **Free space in memory**
                                   (507 Kilobytes)

Check Contiguity of a File

Use this procedure to see whether a file is stored all in one piece on the disk. As you erase and add files, space on the disk is constantly becoming freed or filled in. Adding or modifying long files can break up the information among several different areas of the disk, thus adding to the time it takes for the drive head to access information. To restore file contiguity of a file or files, copy the entire directory to a newly formatted disk (see *FORMAT A FLOPPY DISK* on pages 49–50 and *COPY ALL FILES ON A FLOPPY DISK* on page 47).

1. Insert DOS disk and make that drive current
2. Type **CHKDSK drive:filename**
3. Press **ENTER**
4. If using a single floppy drive system, follow prompts to replace disks

Examples:
    CHKDSK B:MYDATA.DB
    CHKDSK B:*.* (checks all files on Drive B:)

NOTE: Disk and memory information will display followed by the contiguity information for each file you specify.

Display Floppy Disk Volume Label

Use this procedure to view the name of a floppy disk (assigned if disk was formatted with /V parameter or changed with LABEL command).

1. Insert disk in any drive
2. Type **VOL drive:**
3. Press **ENTER**

Change Floppy Disk Volume Label

Use this procedure, available with DOS 3.0 (and above) to create, change, or delete a floppy disk name.

1. Insert DOS disk and make that drive current
2. Type **LABEL drive:**
3. Press **ENTER**
4. If using single floppy drive system, follow prompts to replace disks
5. When current label appears:
   - To create or change label, type **newname** (up to 11 characters) and press **ENTER**, or
   - To delete label, press **ENTER**. At prompt, type **Y**, press **ENTER**.

MANAGING HARD DISKS

Guidelines

- Hard disks are also called fixed disks or rigid disks. They may be built into your computer along with the hard drive or exist in a removable cartridge form.
- A hard disk must be formatted before you can store any files on it. To be able to boot from your hard disk, format the disk and add system files (/S). Once you have formatted a hard disk, do not format it again because formatting erases all the files on the disk.
- You can unformat a hard disk that has been formatted. You can also use the UNFORMAT command to restore a disk that has been corrupted.

Format a Hard Disk

Use this procedure to prepare a new hard disk for use. Also use this procedure to erase all files on a previously used hard disk, reformat the disk, and check for damaged sectors. In order to be able to boot from the hard disk, add system files to your hard disk as indicated in Step 3 below.

NOTE: This procedure erases any programs or data files on your hard disk. Also, to protect yourself from erasing the source disk, place a write-protect tab on your source disk.

1. Insert a DOS disk into Drive A: and make A: current
2. Type **FORMAT C:** (if C: is the hard disk to be formatted)
3. To add system files (makes disk bootable), type **SPACEBAR** /S
4. To add a volume label to the disk, type **SPACEBAR** /V
5. Press **ENTER**
6. If prompted for a label, if desired, type a name for the disk (up to 11 characters), then press **ENTER**

Example: A>**FORMAT C:** /S (formats C: hard disk as bootable disk)

NOTES:
To interrupt formatting before formatting begins, press **CTRL** **BREAK** (or press **CTRL** **C**). To interrupt formatting once it has begun, reboot your computer by pressing **CTRL** **ALT** **DEL** . Once your directory is formatted, files on the disk are not retrievable.

FORMAT ignores assigned (ASSIGN) drives, does not work with network drives, and should not be used with joined (JOIN) and substituted (SUBST) drives.

Check Hard Disk and Memory Status

Use this procedure to view the label and creation date of a disk, the size of the disk, and the amount of free space on the disk. You can also view the current amount of memory available in your computer.

1. Make root directory of hard disk current
2. Type **CHKDSK**
3. If desired, to have CHKDSK correct the directory or File Allocation Table and allow conversion of lost chains to files (named FILEnnnn.CHK), press `SPACEBAR` and type **/F**
4. If desired, to also display all the directories and filenames on the disk, press `SPACEBAR` and type **/V**
5. Press `ENTER`
6. If prompted to "Convert lost chains to files:"
   - If you typed /F in Step 3, you can create new files that contain the lost clusters. Type **Y** and press `ENTER`. Or,
   - To continue without creating new files, type **N** and press `ENTER`

NOTE: If you respond **Y** to Step 6, you will be able to view the lost clusters of ASCII files with your word processor or EDLIN or TYPE their filenames. If the information is no longer useful to you, erase the lost cluster files and thus free more disk space.

Display Hard Disk Volume Label

Use this procedure to view the name of a hard disk. The name was given when the disk was formatted with the /V parameter (see *FORMAT A HARD DISK* procedure on page 54) or LABEL command (see *CHANGE HARD DISK VOLUME LABEL* procedure).

1. With any drive current, type **VOL C:** (if C: contains volume label)
2. Press `ENTER`

Change Hard Disk Volume Label

This procedure (DOS 3.0 and above) manages hard disk names.

1. Make root directory of hard disk current
2. Type **LABEL C:** (if C: contains the volume label)
3. Press `ENTER`
4. When current label appears:
   - To create or change label, type **newname** (up to 11 characters) and press `ENTER`, or
   - To delete label, press `ENTER`. When prompted to confirm deletion, type **Y** and press `ENTER`

CHECKING FOR VIRUSES

Guidelines

- A computer virus is a small program that resides hidden on a disk or in a file. Viruses can multiply and damage information on a disk or purposefully harm programs or data.
- Use MSAV, VSAFE, or Windows Anti-Virus to detect viruses and clean them off your computer. MSAV finds 1000 known viruses.
- When you installed DOS 6.0 on your computer, you had the option of installing Anti-Virus for Windows and MS-DOS, Windows only, MS-DOS only, or None. To use Anti-Virus program in DOS, you had to install it for Windows and MS-DOS or for MS-DOS only.

Check for Viruses

Use Microsoft Anti-Virus to scan memory and specified drives on your computer for viruses. The program will clean the viruses from your computer. This creates a CHKLIST.MS file in each directory. CHKLIST.MS contains checksum information against which to compare subsequent scans of files.

1. Insert DOS disk and make that drive current

2. ■ To display menu-driven program and set the program to scan the current drive, type **MSAV** and press `ENTER`, or
   ■ To display menu-driven program and set the program to scan a specific drive, type **MSAV drive:** and press `ENTER`
3. If menu-driven program appears, to scan a particular drive, select "Select new drive" and follow prompts to select a drive
4. At menu, to change checksum, alarm, backup, report, prompt, or anti-stealth settings, select "Options." When you leave MSAV program, you will be prompted if you want to save these settings.
5. ■ To have computer stop when it finds a virus and prompt you to clean it, select "Detect," or
   ■ To have computer automatically eliminate each virus it finds, select "Detect and Clean"
6. To leave program:
   a. Select "Exit" or press `ESC`
   b. At prompt to save configuration, check box (press `TAB` twice then `SPACEBAR`) if you want to save configuration
   c. Select "OK" or highlight "OK" and press `ENTER`

NOTE: To interrupt scanning of a drive, press `ESC`.

Check for Viruses without Menu
1. Insert DOS disk and make that drive current
2. ▪ To scan Drive C:, type **MSAV C:** **/N** and press **ENTER**, or
   ▪ To scan all drives except Drives A: and B:, type **MSAV** **/N** **/A** and press **ENTER**, or
   ▪ To scan all local drives except network drives, type **MSAV** **/N** **/L** and press **ENTER**

NOTE: You may want to place the **MSAV C:** **/N** or **MSAV** **/N** **/A** or **MSAV** **/N** **/L** commands in your AUTOEXEC.BAT file.

List Viruses that Can be Detected by Microsoft Anti-Virus
1. Insert DOS disk and make that drive current
2. Type **MSAV** and press **ENTER**
3. When menu appears and the program stops reading disk information, press **F9**

Continuously Scan for Viruses
Use this program to continuously monitor your computer for viruses. This memory resident program requires 22K of memory.

1. Make sure that Windows is not running
2. Insert DOS disk and make that drive current
3. Type **VSAFE** and press **ENTER**
4. Virus checking loads into memory and begins monitoring drives and memory for viruses
5. Once VSAFE is loaded into memory, to view VSAFE screen, toggle options on and off, or unload VSAFE from memory, press **ALT** **V**

NOTES:
Do not run Windows installation while VSAFE is in memory.

If running VSAFE before running Windows, add the **LOAD=C:\DOS\MWAVTSR.EXE** command to your WIN.INI file (this allows VSAFE messages to appear in Windows).

DEFRAGMENTING A DISK

Guidelines

- When DOS creates or changes a file, it stores the file in any available free space on a disk. If the file does not fit entirely in the first free space DOS finds, DOS stores just part of the file there and stores the rest of the file in other free areas it finds.
- Use the DEFRAG utility to combine files that are split on different tracks and sectors of a hard or floppy disk. This speeds up disk reading because the drive heads will not need to read different areas of the disk for each file. This is called "optimizing" the disk.
- This command affects all files on disk, but does not affect how files will appear in subdirectories.
- Do not use this command if FASTOPEN is loaded. Do not use this command if Windows is currently running. If Windows is running, fully exit Windows (**ALT** **F** **X**) before typing the command.

Defragment a Hard Disk or Floppy Disk

1. Insert DOS disk and make that drive current
2. Type **DEFRAG** **drive:** and press **ENTER**

3. The screen displays optimization in progress

Examples:
DEFRAG C: (defragments files on Drive C:)
DEFRAG A: (defragments files on disk in Drive A:)

Defragment a Disk with Options

You can specify the drive letter, whether to fully optimize or leave free space between files, and sort the fragmented files by date/time, name, extension, or size. Note that sorting files can increase defragmentation time dramatically.

1. Insert DOS disk and make that drive current
2. Type **DEFRAG** and press **ENTER**
3. To select drive to defragment, press **↑** or **↓** and press **ENTER**
4. After DEFRAG analyzes the disk:
   - To accept recommended method, select "Optimize," or
   - To change method, select "Configure" and change "Optimization Method" or "File sort." To move around dialog box, press **TAB**. To select a button, press **SPACEBAR**. To confirm changes, press **ENTER**. When done, select "Begin optimization."
5. The screen displays optimization in progress

COMPRESSING A DISK (DOUBLESPACE)

Guidelines

- The DoubleSpace program provided by DOS 6.0 enables you to increase the amount of space on a hard or floppy or removable hard disk. DOS accomplishes this by squeezing files into smaller areas on the disk or turning free space into a compressed disk.

- In compressing a disk, DOS maintains the original drive letter specification and creates a new drive letter. The original drive letter refers to the compressed portion of the disk. The new drive letter refers to an uncompressed portion of the drive (now called a host drive) used to retain files that cannot be compressed such as the Windows permanent swap file.

- You can set up a hard disk into several compressed drives. Each drive has a new letter designation.

- Compressing a hard disk does not noticeably slow down disk speed.

- After you have installed DoubleSpace, you can use the program again to create new disks or maintain existing compressed disks. Using advanced DoubleSpace command switches, you can control the size of the compressed disk by how much free space you want it to have, and how much free space you want the host drive to have.

Disadvantages to Using Disk Compression

- You need DOS 6.0 and a computer with DoubleSpace installed to read and write to a compressed floppy disk.

- Once you compress a disk, you cannot uncompress it.

- Compressing a disk may take several hours.

- To recognize compressed drives, DOS loads DBLSPACE.BIN into memory. Once you run DoubleSpace, DOS automatically loads DBLSPACE.BIN as a component of DOS before reading the CONFIG.SYS file. DBLSPACE.BIN requires about 40K of memory. Use DEVICEHIGH=C:\DOS\DBLSPACE.SYS /MOVE command in CONFIG.SYS to move DBLSPACE.BIN into the upper memory area.

Compress a Hard Disk
1. Insert DOS disk and make that drive current
2. Type **DBLSPACE** and press **ENTER**
3. At the Welcome screen, press **ENTER**
4. ■ To compress Drive C: automatically and have the program determine the best settings, select "Express Setup (recommended)" and press **ENTER**, or
   ■ To select the drives to compress and choose your own settings, press ⬇ to select "Custom Setup" and press **ENTER**
   a. Select whether to compress an existing or new, empty drive and press **ENTER**
   b. Select drive to compress and press **ENTER**
   c. When prompted to accept new uncompressed drive setup, you may select a setting and press **ENTER** to select an alternative. Then select "Continue" and press **ENTER**.
   d. To compress drive, type C, or, to return to previous screen, press **ESC**, or, to exit without compressing disk, press **F3**

Compress a Floppy Disk
You can compress a floppy disk whether it is completely empty or contains files. The floppy disk must be formatted and needs to contain at least 200K of free space. To compress a floppy disk, you must have previously installed DoubleSpace on your computer.

1. Insert DOS disk and make that drive current
2. Type **DBLSPACE** /**COMPRESS** **drive:** and press **ENTER**

Example: **DBLSPACE** /**COMPRESS** **A:** (compresses & mounts A:)

Use a Compressed Floppy Disk
You must "mount" a compressed floppy disk before you can use it. The disk is automatically mounted when you first compress the disk. However, if you restart the computer or change disks, use this procedures to mount the floppy disk. To use a compressed floppy disk on another computer, that computer must have had DoubleSpace previously installed.

1. Insert DOS disk and make that drive current
2. Type **DBLSPACE** /**MOUNT** **drive:** and press **ENTER**

Example: **DBLSPACE** /**MOUNT** **A:** (enables reading and writing A:)

BACKING UP HARD DISK

Guidelines

- Even though a hard disk is more resistant to damage than a floppy disk, a hard disk *can* be damaged. For that reason, and because it is possible to inadvertently erase needed files, you should back up your hard disk on a regular basis.
- DOS 6.0 uses a different backup and restore program (MSBACKUP) than previous versions of DOS (which used the BACKUP and RESTORE commands). You cannot use the DOS 6.0 MSBACKUP command to restore files backed up with the BACKUP command.
- Also use BACKUP to copy a long file (that would fill more than one floppy disk) from one hard disk to another.
- You can back up from more than one disk drive during a backup session.
- You can back up onto any DOS-compatible device that is specified by a drive letter: floppy disks, Bernoulli® drives, DOS-compatible tape drives, removable hard disk cartridges, and network drives. If your computer has two floppy disk drives of the same capacity, you can speed up backing up by backing up to both floppy disk drives.
- The floppy disks do not need to be formatted before you back up onto them.
- If the floppy disks contain files, the MSBACKUP command will overwrite the files.
- You can select to compress backup data. This requires fewer floppy disks and can save time in backing up files.
- You can protect backed up data with a password.
- When you installed DOS 6.0 on your computer, you had the option of installing Backup for Windows and MS-DOS, Windows only, MS-DOS only, or None. To use Backup program in DOS, you had to install it for Windows and MS-DOS or for MS-DOS only.
- To use Microsoft Backup for Windows, start up Windows and select the Backup icon from the Microsoft Tools program group.

Full, Incremental, and Differential Backups

- A full backup copies all selected files and sets their archive flags to show that they have been backed up. Use this type of backup to begin a new cycle.
- After making a full backup, choose one of two methods: incremental or differential backups.
- An incremental backup copies all selected files that have been created or modified since the last full or incremental backup and sets their archive flag to show that they have been backed up. Use this type of backup to keep a copy of all data files as they change. You need a new set of backup disks for each incremental backup until you begin the cycle again.
- A differential backup copies all selected files that have been created or modified since the last full backup and does *not* set the archive flag to show that it has been backed up. Use this method if you want to back up all files modified since the full backup. You can reuse the same differential backup disks each time you perform a differential backup.

Monthly Backup Cycle (Incremental)

Week	Method	Effect
1	full	Backs up all files on hard disk and sets each archive flag to show that file was backed up
2	incremental	Backs up the files that have been created or modified since the full backup and sets archive flags to show files are backed up
3	incremental	Backs up the files that have been created or modified since the incremental backup and sets archive flags to show file are backed up
4	incremental	Same as above

Monthly Backup Cycle (Differential)

Week	Method	Effect
1	full	Backs up all files on hard disk and sets each archive flag to show that file was backed up
2	differential	Backs up all files that have been created or modified since the full backup and does not set the archive flags to show that the files have been backed up
3	differential	Same as above
4	differential	Same as above

Setup Files and Catalogs

- Microsoft Backup allows you to save different groups of settings in separate .SET and .SLT "setup" files. Store different drives, directories, individual files, and settings options in setup files. For example, one setup file could include all files on a hard disk and another setup file could include all the files on a network drive.

- Microsoft Backup creates a .CAT "master catalog" file for each setup file you create and stores this file on your hard disk with its associated .SET and .SLT file. The master catalog contains a list of "backup set catalogs." Backup set catalogs record the filenames and locations of individual backups made within the current cycle (since the full backup).

- "Backup set catalogs" of full backups have .FUL extensions, incremental backups have .INC extensions, and differential backups have .DIF extensions.

- When you restore files, select the desired master catalog to restore the most recent versions of all files (the program checks each backup set catalog for the latest version of each file) or to restore an old version of a file (you can choose from a merged list of all versions of all backed up files).

- If you perform a full backup, Microsoft Backup defaults to deleting the "backup set catalogs" and begins a new "backup set catalog." This allows you to begin a new "cycle."

- Cycles set the time period of your backup strategy.

- For example, if you want to perform both monthly and weekly backups of a hard disk drive, first create a setup file that specifies the files to back up (all files). Begin the cycle each month with a full backup (this empties the master catalog and creates a new backup set catalog). As part of this backup strategy, each week you can perform a backup of files created or modified since the previous incremental backup or full backup (called an incremental backup) or a backup of files created or modified since the full backup (called a differential backup). In your strategy, do not mix incremental and differential backups in one cycle. Incremental or differential backups each week will add backup set catalogs to the master catalog. Each new month, start a new cycle by performing a full backup — you can use the original full backup disks.

- In case your hard disk is damaged, it is a good idea to keep a copy of your master catalog (.CAT) and all associated catalogs on a floppy disk.

Moving Around Backup Dialog Box

Move to next item	**TAB**
Move to previous item	**SHIFT** **TAB**
Move within a list box	↑ ↓
Leave a list box	**TAB**

Using a Mouse

Activate button	**CLICK** or **CLICK**
Select from menu	**CLICK** or **CLICK**
Select all files on a drive	**CLICK** on drive in Backup From
Select directory or file from list	**CLICK** or **CLICK2X**
De-select	**CLICK** or **CLICK2X**
Select multiple directories or files from a list	**DRAG**
Scroll through list	**DRAG** up/down
Cancel operation, close dialog box	**CLICK2X** top left corner

Selecting in Backup Dialog Box

Select a hotkey	press highlighted letter
Select from a menu	hold down **ALT**, press letter
Select hotkey in a list box	hold down **ALT**, press letter
Change a check mark box, radio button, and list item	**SPACEBAR**
Select all files on a drive	select drive letter from Backup From drive list
Select directory or file from a list	**SPACEBAR**
De-select	**SPACEBAR**
Select default button (with > <)	**ENTER**
When finished with dialog box	select OK
Cancel operation, close dialog box	**ESC** or select Cancel
Context sensitive help	**F1**

Back up Hard Disk (Full Backup)

Use this procedure to start a new backup cycle.

1. Insert DOS disk and make that drive current
2. Type **MSBACKUP** and press `ENTER`
3. If this is the first time you are using this command on this computer, you will be asked to have backup configure itself for that computer. At prompt, select "Start Configuration." To change an option from the dialog box, to move to desired item, press `TAB`. To change a check mark box, press `SPACEBAR`. To change a button such as "Double-Click," select button and press `ENTER`. When finished with a dialog box, select OK. When configuration and drive testing is complete, select "Save."
4. To select a pre-established backup setup (such as entire C: drive), press `ALT` `F` (File) and select "Open Setup"
5. To back up hard disk, select "Backup"
6. At dialog box, select files to back up under "Backup From." To select all files in a drive, `CLICK2X` the drive (or select and press `ENTER` at the drive name), or, to select specific files and/or directories, select "Select Files" button.
7. Select "Backup To" and select drive to contain backed up files.

Select "MS-DOS Drive and Path" if not backing up to floppy disks or to an IBM XT with a 1.2MB drive controller and type a drive specifier and optional pathname.

8. To change options such as verification, compression, password, prompt before overwriting used diskettes, always formatting diskettes, using error correction on diskettes, keeping old backup catalogs, and beeping on prompts, select "Options." Verification can substantially slow down backing up.
9. If desired, to save the current file selections, backup settings, and options, from the pull-down menu, select File then select Save Setup (or Save Setup As and type a new name for the .SET file)
10. To select a full backup, select "Backup Type" and "Full"
11. When settings are complete, select "Start Backup"

Back up Hard Disk (Incremental or Differential Backup)

Use this procedure once you have begun a backup cycle with the previous procedure.

1. Insert DOS disk and make that drive current
2. Type **MSBACKUP** and press **ENTER**
3. To select a pre-established backup setup (such as entire C: drive), press **ALT** **F** (File) and select "Open Setup"
4. To back up hard disk, select "Backup"
5. Select "Backup To" and select drive to contain backed up files. Select "MS-DOS Drive and Path" if not backing up to floppy disks or to an IBM XT with a 1.2MB drive controller and type a drive specifier and optional pathname.
6. To change options such as verification, compression, password, prompt before overwriting used diskettes, always formatting diskettes, using error correction on diskettes, keeping old backup catalogs, and beeping on prompts, select "Options." Verification can substantially slow down backing up.
7. To make an incremental or differential backup, select "Backup Type" then "Incremental" or "Differential." The program will only back up those files whose archive flag indicates that it has not been backed up yet.
8. When settings are complete, select "Start Backup"

Compare Backed Up Files with Hard Disk

Use this procedure to verify that the backup floppy disks contain exact copies of the backed up files on the hard disk. This tests whether a backup proceeded without errors.

1. Insert DOS disk and make that drive current
2. Type **MSBACKUP** and press **ENTER**
3. Select "Compare"
4. Select "Backup Set Catalog" and select catalog to compare
5. To select all files in a drive, **CLICKON** the drive (or select and press **ENTER** at the drive name), or, to select specific files and/or directories, select "Select Files" button.
6. Select "Compare From" and select drive containing disks with backup files
7. Select "Start Compare"
8. The Compare Progress screen appears as files are compared

Restore Backed Up Files to Hard Disk

Use this procedure to restore backed up files from floppy disk(s) to the original or a new hard disk.

1. Insert DOS disk and make that drive current
2. Type **MSBACKUP** and press `ENTER`
3. To select a pre-established backup setup (such as entire C: drive), press `ALT` `F` (File) and select "Open Setup"
4. Select "Restore"
5. To select a catalog, select "Backup Set Catalog." If catalog is on a different disk, select "Catalog" button (this button is also useful for retrieving a catalog stored on the last disk of a set of backed up disks).
6. To restore all files in catalog, `CLICK2X` drive letter in "Restore Files" or, to select a subgroup of backed up files, select "Select Files" button
7. Select destination of files to restore at "Restore To." If you select to restore the file(s) to other drives or directories, at Step 9 you will be asked for a new drive or directory name.
8. To change verification, prompting, and restoring of empty directories, select "Options"
9. To begin restoring, select "Start Restore" button
10. During restore operation, if desired to cancel restoring, select "Cancel" or press `ESC`

Configure New Hardware for Backup

If you add drives to your computer, remove drives from your computer, change the monitor type, or want to change mouse speed, sensitivity, or left-handed usage, follow this procedure.

1. Insert DOS disk and make that drive current
2. Type **MSBACKUP** and press `ENTER`
3. Select "Configure"
4. If desired, select "Video and Mouse" and change options
5. If desired, select "Backup Devices" and either select type of drives that are on your computer or press "Auto Config" button for Backup to determine the types of drives on your computer
6. If desired, to confirm that Backup can use your floppy drive (no other backup medium available in this test), select "Compatibility Test"
7. When finished configuring backup and performing Compatibility Test, select "Save" button

LINKING TWO COMPUTERS

Guidelines
- Using the InterInk program, you can link two computers together:
  - You can share files between the computers without having to copy files onto floppy disks. This is useful if you own a laptop computer that does not have floppy disks, if you have two computers with incompatible floppy disk drives, or if you routinely share files between two computers.
  - You can run programs from one computer on another computer.
  - You can share printers, so if one computer is attached to a printer, the other computer can print to that printer.
- To share files directly, you need to link the two computers together with a cable. Attach the cable to both computers' parallel ports or to both computers' serial ports. A parallel port has 25 pins. A serial port has either 9 or 25 pins. Use a bidirectional parallel cable, a 3-wire serial cable, or a 7-wire null modem serial cable.
- One computer will become the client and the other becomes the server. Make the laptop the client or the computer with the printer the server. When the two computers are connected, you will type all commands that affect both computers on the client computer (e.g., the laptop). Meanwhile, the server computer will display the status of the connection.
- As you type on the client, you will have access to more drives than your normal drives on that computer. These additional drives correspond to the drives on the server computer. For example, if you normally have just Drives A: and C:, you may now have an additional D:, E:, and F:.
- Note that you cannot switch between tasks in Windows or DOSSHELL while InterInk is running.

Link Two Computers Together

1. Attach cable to both computers' parallel ports or serial ports
2. To set up client computer to link:
   a. Display client computer's CONFIG.SYS file in Edit, Edlin, or your word processing program in ASCII mode
   b. Add one of the lines listed on page 70 to the CONFIG.SYS file depending on the port to which the cable is attached. Position the line after any other commands that affect drives such as network, RAM disk, or Bernoulli® disk drivers.
   c. Save and exit the modified CONFIG.SYS file
   d. Restart the client computer by pressing **CTRL** **ALT** **DEL**
3. On the server computer:
   a. Insert DOS disk and make that drive current
   b. Type **INTERSVR** and press **ENTER**. This makes all drives available to the client computer. To limit access to server or to direct client drive requests, see page 117.
4. On the client computer:
   a. Insert DOS disk and make that drive current
   b. Type **INTERLNK** and press **ENTER**. This makes the client's next drive specifier refer to the server's first available drive. To set which server drive the client's specifier should refer to, see page 117.
5. The computers will be connected. From the client (e.g., laptop computer) you can copy files, run programs, and print on the server computer. For example, to copy a file from the client's Drive A: to the server's Drive C:, you may type **COPY A:filename D:**.

Options for Adding INTERLNK.EXE to CONFIG.SYS

DEVICE=C:\DOS\INTERLNK.EXE (Interlnk scans all serial and parallel ports for port connected to server)
DEVICE=C:\DOS\INTERLNK.EXE **/LPT** (Interlnk scans all parallel ports for server)
DEVICE=C:\DOS\INTERLNK.EXE **/COM** (Interlnk scans all serial ports for server)
DEVICE=C:\DOS\INTERLNK.EXE **/LPT:2** (Interlnk transfers files through the second parallel port)
DEVICE=C:\DOS\INTERLNK.EXE **/COM:1** (Interlnk transfers files through the first serial port)
DEVICE=C:\DOS\INTERLNK.EXE **/COM:3F8** (Interlnk transfers files through a non-standard serial port where 3F8 is the port address)
DEVICE=C:\DOS\INTERLNK.EXE **/AUTO** (installs Interlnk device driver only if the computer can establish a connection with the server during startup)
DEVICE=C:\DOS\INTERLNK.EXE **/DRIVES:4** (specifies that client can access 4 remote drives rather than the default of 3 drives)
DEVICE=C:\DOS\INTERLNK.EXE **/NOPRINTER** (does not re-route print requests — useful if you want to continue using the client's printer)
DEVICE=C:\DOS\INTERLNK.EXE **/V** (prevents conflict with computer's timer — add this switch if server stops running when you access a drive or printer through Interlnk)
DEVICE=C:\DOS\INTERLNK.EXE **/LOW** (loads Interlnk device driver into conventional memory — even if you do not use the DEVICEHIGH command, DOS places Interlnk in upper memory area if UMB is set up and memory is available)
DEVICE=C:\DOS\INTERLNK.EXE **/LPT:2 /AUTO /DRIVES:5 /NOPRINTER** (combines options)

Display Status of InterInk

1. On client computer, insert DOS disk and make that drive current
2. Type **INTERLNK** and press `ENTER`
3. A screen appears showing the port used to connect the computers and displaying a list of which server drives are available and which server printer ports are available to the client

NOTE: While the two computers are connected, the server displays the status of the connection on its screen.

Break Connection

1. To break link, on server computer's keyboard, press jALTk jF4k
2. To restart connection, on server computer's keyboard, type **INTERSVR** and press `ENTER`

Re-establish Connection

1. If the server is running:
   - Whenever you restart the client, the computers connect, or
   - Type **INTERLNK** on the client computer and press `ENTER`, or
   - Log into one of the server's drives from the client computer

Copy InterInk Files to Another Computer

Use this procedure if only one computer has the InterInk program and you cannot use floppy disks to copy the files to the other computer.

1. Connect both computers via their serial ports with a 7-wire null modem serial cable. If you cannot connect the cable to the COM1 port on the computer to copy files to, make sure that the SHARE program is not loaded; if it is loaded, remove it from the AUTOEXEC.BAT file and restart the computer.
2. Make sure the computer to receive the files has the MODE.COM file in its Path
3. On computer to receive the files, log into directory to contain files (e.g., **A:** or **CD \DOS**)
4. On computer to send the files, type **INTERSVR /RCOPY** and press `ENTER`
5. Follow instructions on the screen to copy the files

CONFIGURATION PROCEDURES

CREATING BOOT DISKS

Create a Bootable Floppy Disk

Use this procedure If you wish to boot with a floppy disk. A boot disk must contain system "tracks" (formatted sectors), hidden files, and a COMMAND.COM file, and may also contain an AUTOEXEC.BAT file which is automatically executed every time you boot your computer.

1. ■ To create from a floppy disk, insert a DOS disk into Drive A: and make Drive A: current, or
   ■ You can create from any drive or directory on a hard disk as long as the PATH statement points to the DOS directory
2. Insert a new unformatted disk or a previously used disk (will be erased) into Drive B: or you can use Drive A: to create from a hard disk
3. If the floppy disk to create as a bootable disk is in:
   ■ Drive A:, type **FORMAT A: /S**, or
   ■ Drive B:, type **FORMAT B: /S**
4. Press ENTER

5. When asked to confirm, make sure that you are formatting the disk in the correct drive, and press ENTER
6. It may take over a minute to format the disk and add the DOS system (/S) files
7. If desired, create an AUTOEXEC.BAT file and store on new boot disk (see *CREATE AN AUTOEXEC.BAT FILE* procedure on page 24). If you have disk space available, you may store other DOS or program files on your boot disk.

NOTE: To create a bootable floppy disk from a disk that has already been formatted (can contain files), follow *ADD A NEW DOS VERSION* procedure on page 73.

Create a Bootable Hard Disk

1. Follow *FORMAT A HARD DISK* procedure on page 54 using the /S parameter described in that procedure

CONFIGURE

View DOS Version Number

Use this procedure to view which version of the operating system is currently running. Some procedures in this guide only apply to a particular version of DOS.

1. Type **VER**
2. Press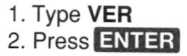

Add a New DOS Version

Use this procedure to upgrade a boot disk from one DOS version to another or to add system files to a blank, formatted disk. SYS will not work on all versions of DOS, all computers, and all disk drives. You may need to reformat the disk.

1. Boot computer with DOS disk containing new DOS version
2. Make drive from which you booted current
3. Type **SYS target drive:** and press **ENTER**
4. If using a single floppy drive system, if prompted, replace DOS disk with disk to contain new version and press **ENTER**. When operation is complete, place DOS disk back into Drive A:.
5. Type **COPY A:COMMAND.COM target drive:** (if A: contains new DOS version) and press **ENTER**. NOTE: Skip Step 5 for later versions of DOS. It automatically copies COMMAND.COM.
6. If using a single floppy drive system, if prompted, replace DOS disk with disk to contain new version and press **ENTER**

CONFIGURING YOUR OPERATING SYSTEM

Guidelines
- There are various ways in which you can increase the ease of use of your operating system.
- You must also perform some necessary configuration procedures so that DOS knows where to find important operating system files and program files.

View DOS Environment
Use this procedure to view a listing of the current PROMPT and PATH and to view the location of the COMMAND.COM (or other command processor) file

1. Type **SET**
2. Press **ENTER**

Modify Directory Path
1. To create, view, or delete the directory PATH, see procedures on pages 19-20

Modify System Prompt

Use this procedure if you want to include a message in, or modify the appearance of, the DOS prompt (e.g., C>, A>).

1. Type **PROMPT text and/or parameters** (see table and example on this page)
2. Press **ENTER**

NOTES:
You can include as many parameters as desired. Precede each parameter with a dollar sign ($). Do not precede text with a $ (see example).

If necessary, to exit once you have begun to modify the prompt, press **CTRL** **BREAK** (or press **CTRL** **C**).

Return to Normal System Prompt

Use this procedure to change the system prompt back to the default (A>) format.

1. Type **PROMPT**
2. Press **ENTER**

Prompt Command Parameters

PARAMETER	RESULT	PARAMETER	RESULT
$d	Current date	$q	= sign
$t	Current time	$b	| sign
$n	Current drive	$$	$ sign
$p	Current directory path	$e	Escape character
$v	DOS version	$h	Backspace
$g	> sign	$_	Carriage return/ line feed
$l	< sign		

Example of Modified Prompt

Type:
PROMPT Time is t_Directory is p_ng
Result:
Time is 11:43:14.67
Directory is C:\WRITEIT\NOTES
C>

Modify System Date

DOS stamps the system date and time on any newly created or modified file. This is useful for organizing files and performing the BACKUP command. Use this procedure to view or modify the date recognized by DOS. If your computer has a built-in clock, refer to your computer operator's manual for instructions on resetting the clock.

1. Type **DATE**
2. Press **ENTER**
3. When system date appears:
   - To change date, type a new date using **MM–DD–YY** or **MM–DD–YYYY** format and press **ENTER** , or
   - To accept default date, press **ENTER**

NOTES:
You are prompted for a system date and time when you boot your computer unless you have an AUTOEXEC.BAT file on your boot disk. If you are using an AUTOEXEC.BAT file and do not have a built-in clock, you should place the DATE and TIME commands in the AUTOEXEC.BAT file so that the system will prompt you for the date and time.

With most DOS versions, you may use a / or . (period) instead of a – when specifying a new date. You can also change the system date by typing the date as a parameter after the verb DATE.

Examples:
DATE 5–16–93
DATE 5–16–1993
DATE 5.16.93
DATE 5.16.1993
DATE 5/16/93
DATE 5/16/93

Modify System Time

Use this procedure to view or modify the time recognized by DOS. DOS uses a 24-hour clock. Add 12 hours to the p.m. time to give the 24-hour time. For example, if the time is 4:01 p.m., when prompted for the time, type 16:01. If your computer has a built-in clock, refer to the appropriate manual for instructions on resetting the clock.

1. Type **TIME**
2. Press **ENTER**
3. When system time appears:
   - To change time, type a new time using **HH:MM:SS.hundredths** format. You may specify only a portion (the beginning part) of the time if you wish. Then press **ENTER**. Or,
   - To accept default time, press **ENTER**

NOTES:
You are prompted for a system date and time when you boot your computer unless you have an AUTOEXEC.BAT file on your boot disk. If you are using an AUTOEXEC.BAT file and do not have a built-in clock, you should place the DATE and TIME commands in the AUTOEXEC.BAT file and the system will prompt you for the date and time.

With most DOS versions, you may use a . (period) instead of a : (colon) when specifying a new time. You can also change the system time by typing a new time as a parameter after the verb TIME.

Examples
   TIME 9:15:30
   TIME 13:48
   TIME 9.15.30
   TIME 16.3

Specify New Location of Command Processor

DOS must know where COMMAND.COM (the command processor) is stored at all times. Many application programs replace the transient portion of COMMAND.COM while they are running and then need to reload it upon exiting.

Specify the location of COMMAND.COM if you boot with and then remove one disk, but have another disk present (such as a hard disk or RAM disk) which also contains a copy of COMMAND.COM.

1. ■ To set a new location for COMMAND.COM for the current session, but not execute an AUTOEXEC.BAT file on the new drive, follow *SET COMSPEC* procedure, or
   ■ To activate COMMAND.COM again, specify the new location, and execute AUTOEXEC.BAT or another specified file, follow *ACTIVATE COMMAND.COM* procedure on page 79, or
   ■ To specify a different command processor or specify a new location for future sessions (in CONFIG.SYS file), follow *SPECIFY NEW SHELL* procedure on page 82

Set COMSPEC

Use this procedure to set a new location for COMMAND.COM without executing an AUTOEXEC.BAT file in the new directory.

1. Type **SET COMSPEC=full pathname**
2. Press **ENTER**

Example: **SET COMSPEC=C:\COMMAND.COM**

Activate COMMAND.COM

This procedure re-activates COMMAND.COM, specifies the new
location, and executes AUTOEXEC.BAT or another specified file.

1. Insert DOS disk and make that drive current
2. Type **COMMAND directory name**
3. If desired, to permanently erase command processor in memory
   and run AUTOEXEC.BAT in root, press **SPACEBAR** and type **/P**
4. Press **ENTER**

Example: **COMMAND C:\ /P**

NOTE: If you did not type /P, to exit new command processor, type
EXIT and press **ENTER**. To activate a new file or command,

type **/C**.

Example: **COMMAND C:\ /C TEXT**

USING CONFIG.SYS

Guidelines

- Your CONFIG.SYS file is a small file, containing only ASCII characters, into which you can type several memory usage and file location commands. Store the CONFIG.SYS file in the root directory of the boot disk.
- CONFIG.SYS commands affect how quickly DOS will work, how many files you can have open simultaneously, and where DOS will find the command processor and device driver files.
- Changes you make to your CONFIG.SYS file will not take effect immediately. To make the changes effective, reboot your computer. When you reboot, DOS reads the new CONFIG.SYS file before it reads the AUTOEXEC.BAT file.

Create a CONFIG.SYS File

1. If you do not already have a CONFIG.SYS file on your boot disk, you can easily create one with your word processing program in ASCII mode, EDLIN, or EDIT. Create a file named CONFIG.SYS in the root directory of the boot disk, and type in any of the necessary commands in the procedures that follow. Type one command per line, each command aligned on the left margin. The file can only contain ASCII characters.

Modify CONFIG.SYS File

1. Use your word processing program in ASCII mode, EDLIN, or EDIT to modify the CONFIG.SYS file.

View CONFIG.SYS File

1. ■ If desired, use your word processing program in ASCII mode, EDLIN, or EDIT to view and modify the CONFIG.SYS file, or
   ■ To quickly view the file, type **TYPE drive:CONFIG.SYS** and press **ENTER**

Sample CONFIG.SYS File

```
files=20
buffers=15
device=c:\dos\ansi.sys
device=c:\windows\mouse.sys
```

Modify Number of Open Files Available
(DEFAULT = 8, MAXIMUM = 99)

Use this procedure to allow DOS to have more than 8 files open at one time. This is useful for programs that use several open files simultaneously.

1. View CONFIG.SYS with your word processing program in ASCII mode, EDLIN, or EDIT
2. If no line lists the number of files, then the default of a maximum of 8 files is in effect. To enable DOS to open more files, type **FILES=number** on a separate line.

Example: **FILES=20**

NOTE: Minimum number of files is 5. Each file over 8 increases the space DOS uses in memory by 48 bytes.

Modify Number of Disk Buffers
(DEFAULT = 2–3, MAXIMUM = 99)

Use this procedure to change the number of memory buffers DOS will use. A memory buffer is an area of memory where DOS stores directory listings, overlay files, and parts of working files. The more buffers you make available to DOS, the faster DOS (and any programs that randomly read and write to disk) will operate. Too many buffers, however, slow down DOS and take too much memory.

1. View CONFIG.SYS with your word processing program in ASCII mode, EDLIN, or EDIT
2. If no line lists the number of buffers, then the default of 2 or 3 buffers is in effect. To add more buffers, type **BUFFERS=number** on a separate line.

Example: **BUFFERS=15**

NOTES:
10–15 is a reasonable number of buffers for a computer with 256K–640K memory. Test out different numbers of buffers to see what number makes your computer and software perform the fastest.

Each buffer over 2–3 increases the space DOS uses in memory by 528 bytes.

Add Device Drivers

When you add peripheral components to your computer, you often need to provide DOS with a driver file that tells DOS how to access the device. Devices can be a RAM disk, disk cache, mouse, etc. This procedure invokes the device driver and specifies its location.

1. View CONFIG.SYS with your word processing program in ASCII mode, EDLIN, or EDIT
2. On a separate line, type **DEVICE=filename.ext**

Example: **DEVICE=C:DOS\DRIVERS\ANSI.SYS**

Turn Break On/Off
(DEFAULT = Off)

Use this procedure to turn **BREAK** on as a default; that is, to have DOS look for the keyboard-issued **CTRL** **BREAK** (**CTRL** **C**) command during all operations. With BREAK off, DOS only looks for **CTRL** **BREAK** (**CTRL** **C**) while using the keyboard, monitor, printer, or serial ports. Turn BREAK on when your programs have prolonged disk-access activities and you need to halt operations.

1. View CONFIG.SYS with your word processing program in ASCII mode, EDLIN, or EDIT
2. ▪ To turn BREAK on, type **BREAK=ON**, or
   ▪ To turn BREAK off, type **BREAK=OFF**

NOTE: This has the same effect as the **BREAK ON/OFF** command.

Specify New Shell

See *SPECIFY NEW LOCATION OF COMMAND PROCESSOR* procedure on page 78.

Use this procedure to specify a command processor or specify a location for COMMAND.COM. AUTOEXEC.BAT will not automatically run, nor will the new command processor be reloaded upon exiting other programs unless you also follow *SET COMSPEC* procedure.

1. View CONFIG.SYS with your word processing program in ASCII mode, EDLIN, or EDIT
2. On a separate line, type **SHELL=filename full pathname**
3. If desired, to have DOS remove the current command processor from memory as well, press **SPACEBAR** and type **/P**
4. Save CONFIG.SYS file and reboot computer

Example: **SHELL=COMMAND.COM C:\DOS /P**

BYPASSING CONFIG.SYS

Guidelines

- You can start your computer without its reading the CONFIG.SYS and AUTOEXEC.BAT files. This gives your computer a basic configuration of the following:
  ```
  PATH=C:\DOS
  PROMPT=$P$G
  COMSPEC=C:\COMMAND.COM
  ```

- You can start your computer and accept or reject each CONFIG.SYS command in turn and run or choose not to run the AUTOEXEC.BAT file.

- To giver the user a choice of CONFIG.SYS and AUTOEXEC.BAT options when booting your computer, see **CREATING A MENU OF OPTIONS FOR CONFIG.SYS** section on page 84.

Start Computer without CONFIG.SYS and AUTOEXEC.BAT

1. Turn on computer or restart computer with `CTRL` `ALT` `DEL`
2. When "Starting MS-DOS..." displays on the screen either press `F5` (Stop Startup) or hold down `SHIFT`
3. DOS will start without loading CONFIG.SYS or running AUTOEXEC.BAT and the DOS prompt (C>) will appear

Start Computer and Accept or Reject CONFIG.SYS Commands

1. Turn on computer or restart computer with `CTRL` `ALT` `DEL`
2. When "Starting MS-DOS..." displays on the screen press `F8` (Step Startup)
3. DOS will prompt you to accept or reject each CONFIG.SYS command in turn:
   - To confirm displayed command, type Y, or
   - To not execute command, type N
4. When prompted "Process AUTOEXEC.BAT:"
   - To run AUTOEXEC.BAT, type Y, or
   - To bypass running AUTOEXEC.BAT, type N
5. The DOS prompt (C>) will appear

NOTE: You can have your computer prompt you to confirm a CONFIG.SYS command by typing a ? before = in a command (e.g., DOS?=HIGH). To add ? to your CONFIG.SYS file, edit CONFIG.SYS file with a word processing program in ASCII mode, EDLIN, or EDIT.

CREATING MENUS IN CONFIG.SYS

Guidelines

- You can create a menu within CONFIG.SYS to prompt the user to choose a configuration.

- Before modifying CONFIG.SYS and AUTOEXEC.BAT files, run DOS command MEMMAKER to maximize use of your memory.

- You may want to copy your CONFIG.SYS and AUTOEXEC.BAT files to a bootable floppy disk, modify the files on the disk, and restart your computer using that disk. After testing the new files, back up your existing CONFIG.SYS and AUTOEXEC.BAT files and copy the new versions to the root of your boot drive (e.g., C.\).

- Use the following commands. Each command is optional except MENUITEM:

Menu Commands in CONFIG.SYS

```
MENUITEM=blockname[,menutext]
MENUDEFAULT=blockname[,timeout]
MENUCOLOR=x[,y]
SUBMENU=blockname[,menutext]
INCLUDE=blockname
NUMLOCK=ON or OFF
```

Menu Colors Available

0	Black	4	Red	8	Gray	12	Bright Red
1	Blue	5	Magenta	9	Bright Blue	13	Bright Magenta
2	Green	6	Brown	10	Bright Green	14	Yellow
3	Cyan	7	White	11	Bright Cyan	15	Bright White

Create Menu of CONFIG.SYS Choices

1. Edit CONFIG.SYS file with your word processing program in ASCII mode, EDLIN, or EDIT
2. Structure file as follows:
   - Type **[menu]**.
   - Type a list of **menuitems** referring to configuration block heads. The head can be any length, but cannot contain spaces. To have a different description appear for the user, type a comma after the head and type a description which may include spaces. Also use these heads in an AUTOEXEC.BAT file if you wish to only execute certain commands upon booting (requires **goto %config%** statement in AUTOEXEC.BAT file and **:head** followed by commands to execute - see page 87).
   - If desired, type **submenu** and a configuration block head. This head will refer to a block of further menuitems or submenus, allowing you to create several levels of menus.
   - If desired, type **menudefault** if you would like DOS to pick a menuitem if the user does not respond. If you do not type a menudefault, the first menuitem is the default if the user pressed **ENTER**. If you type a menudefault and a comma and a timeout, the default will execute after the specified number of seconds if the user does not make a selection. You can type a timeout of 0-90 seconds. If you type a menudefault but no timeout, the default will execute automatically if the user presses **ENTER**.
   - If desired, type **menucolor**, followed by foreground and optional background colors. DOS remains in these colors. See page 84.
   - Type **[common]** and list CONFIG.SYS commands to execute no matter what choice the user makes.
   - Also add the **[common]** line to the end of the CONFIG.SYS file for applications that might add configuration commands to the end of CONFIG.SYS. These commands will be in common for all configuration options.
   - Type each menuitem or submenu **head** in brackets followed by the commands to be executed under that configuration. In additional to normal CONFIG.SYS commands, you may use the following unique commands:
     - **INCLUDE=blockname**. This includes the CONFIG.SYS commands from another configuration block.
     - **NUMLOCK=ON** (or OFF). This turns **NUM LOCK** key on or off. You can only use this command in a configuration block.

Example of a CONFIG.SYS File with Options

```
[menu]
MENUITEM=Fred, Begin DOS
MENUITEM=Dorothy, Begin Windows
SUBMENU=Plain, Your Choice of Plain DOS or Windows
MENUDEFAULT=Dorothy, 30
MENUCOLOR=14,1

[common]
BUFFERS=24,0
FILES=70

[Fred]
NUMLOCK=ON
SHELL=C:\DOS\COMMAND.COM C:\DOS\ /P

[Dorothy]
INCLUDE=Fred
DEVICE=C:\DOS\HIMEM.SYS
DEVICE=C:\DOS\EMM386.EXE NOEMS WIN=ED00-EFFF
  WIN=EA00 ECFF
DOS=UMB
```

```
FCBS=4,0
DEVICEHIGH /L:1,12048 =C:\DOS\SETVER.EXE
DOS=HIGH
STACKS=9,256

[Plain]
MENUITEM=Do_DOS, Run plain DOS
MENUITEM=Do_Windows, Run plain Windows

[Do_DOS]

[Do_Windows]
DEVICE=C:\DOS\HIMEM.SYS

[common]
```

Menu Created by CONFIG.SYS File

```
MS-DOS 6 Startup Menu
-----------------------------------

    1. Begin DOS
    2. Begin Windows
    3. Your Choice of Plain DOS or Windows
```

Example of AUTOEXEC.BAT File with Different Configuration Options

```
@ECHO OFF
PROMPT $P$G
SET DIRCMD=/P /OGEN /A
GOTO %CONFIG%

:Fred
PATH C:\DOS;C:\;C:\DOS\UTILS
C:\WINDOWS\LMOUSE.COM
GOTO End

:Dorothy
PATH C:\DOS;C:\SHEETS\EXCEL;C:\WINDOWS;C:\
LH /L:0;1,42384 /S C:\DOS\SMARTDRV.EXE
LH /L:1,35184 C:\WINDOWS\LMOUSE.COM
SET TEMP=C:\WINDOWS\TEMP
WIN
GOTO End

:Do_DOS
GOTO End

:Do_Windows
C:\WINDOWS\WIN
GOTO End

:End
```

MANAGING MEMORY

MAXIMIZING MEMORY (MEMMAKER)

Guidelines

- Use the MEMMAKER program to optimize your computer's use of memory. This procedure only works on 80386 and higher computers with extended memory.

- MEMMAKER determines if it can move device drivers and memory-resident programs into the upper memory area (the 640K to 1024K region between conventional and extended memory).

- If MEMMAKER can improve upper memory area usage, it modifies your CONFIG.SYS and AUTOEXEC.BAT files and possibly your Windows' SYSTEM.INI file. MEMMAKER stores the old versions of these files. Whenever you start your computer, the new settings in these files take effect.

- Running MEMMAKER frees up room in conventional memory. This means that you can have more and larger programs in memory, and programs that use extended memory can run faster.

Run MEMMAKER Program

Do not run the MEMMAKER program while Windows is running.

1. Insert DOS disk and make that drive current
2. Type **MEMMAKER** and press `ENTER`
3. Follow instructions on the screen

NOTE: If you need to restore your CONFIG.SYS, AUTOEXEC.BAT, and SYSTEM.INI files to the state they were in before you began MEMMAKER, type **MEMMAKER** /**UNDO** and press `ENTER`.

MAXIMIZE MEMORY IN 80386 and 80486

Guidelines

- CONFIG.SYS files using the HIMEM.SYS command should have shadow RAM turned off via the computer's setup utility or (on some computers) via /shadowram:off switch in the HIMEM.SYS command.
- The phrase "physically present expanded memory" means that a memory board using the LIM EMS specification (Lotus-Intel-Microsoft) has been added to your computer.
- If you are using your own expanded memory driver (instead of EMM386.EXE), your driver might require a slightly different configuration.

386 or 486 with extended memory and no physically present expanded memory (see UMA on page 91 for optimizing)

CONFIG.SYS
```
files=20
buffers=10
device=c:\dos\himem.sys
dos=high
device=c:\dos\emm386.exe ram
```
(*This optional driver simulates expanded memory from extended memory. Or, you can use another simulator, e.g., Windows' built-in simulator.*)
```
install=fastopen.exe c:=30
```

AUTOEXEC.BAT
```
c:\dos\smartdrv.exe 1024
```

386 or 486 with extended memory and physically present expanded memory

CONFIG.SYS
```
files=20
buffers=10
device=c:\dos\himem.sys
dos=high
device=your expanded memory driver
install=fastopen.exe c:=100 /x
```

AUTOEXEC.BAT
```
c:\dos\smartdrv.exe 2048
```

MAXIMIZE MEMORY IN 8088 and 80286

Guideline

■ The phrase "physically present expanded memory" means that a memory board using the LIM EMS specification (Lotus-Intel-Microsoft) has been added to your computer.

8088 or 286-with physically present expanded memory and no extended memory

CONFIG.SYS   files=20
    buffers=10
    device=your expanded memory driver
    install=fastopen.exe c:=100 /x

8088 or 286 with physically present expanded memory and extended memory

CONFIG.SYS   files=20
    buffers=10
    device=c:\dos\himem.sys
    dos=high
    device=your expanded memory driver
    install=fastopen.exe c:=100 /x

AUTOEXEC.BAT   c:\dos\smartdrv.exe 2048

8088 or 286 with extended memory and no physically present expanded memory
(Shadow RAM turned *on* via computer's setup utility)

CONFIG.SYS   files=20
    buffers=10
    install=fastopen.exe c:=30

(Shadow RAM turned *off* via computer's setup utility)

CONFIG.SYS   files=20
    buffers=10
    device=c:\dos\himem.sys
    dos=high
    install=fastopen.exe c:=30

AUTOEXEC.BAT   c:\dos\smartdrv.exe 1024

USING UPPER MEMORY AREA

Guidelines

- Upper memory area is the area of memory between conventional memory and the high memory area. It occupies the 640K to 1024K region. Your computer normally uses the upper memory area for hardware buffers (e.g., the screen). If there is available space in this area, DOS can place itself, devices, and programs there.
- Your computer's shadow RAM should be turned off via the computer's setup utility.
- The computer must have extended memory.

386 or 486 with extended memory

CONFIG.SYS	device=c:\dos\himem.sys
	dos=high,umb
	device=c:\dos\emm386.exe noems
	devicehigh=load other drivers
AUTOEXEC.BAT	loadhigh programname
	loadhigh c:\dos\smartdrv.exe 1024
	loadhigh c:\dos\fastopen.exe c:=100

386 or 486 with extended memory set up to simulate expanded memory

CONFIG.SYS	device=c:\dos\himem.sys
	dos=high,umb
	device=c:\dos\emm386.exe ram
	devicehigh=load other drivers
AUTOEXEC.BAT	loadhigh programname
	loadhigh c:\dos\smartdrv.exe 512
	loadhigh c:\dos\fastopen.exe c:=40 /x

386 or 486 with extended memory and physically present expanded memory

CONFIG.SYS	device=c:\dos\himem.sys
	dos=high,umb
	device=your expanded memory driver
	devicehigh=load other drivers
AUTOEXEC.BAT	loadhigh programname
	loadhigh c:\dos\smartdrv.exe 2048
	loadhigh c:\dos\fastopen.exe c:=40 /x

REDIRECTING AND PIPING INFORMATION

Guidelines

- Programs and DOS commands normally receive needed information from the keyboard and display the results on the video screen. The keyboard is the *standard input* device and the video screen is the *standard output* device.

- There are occasions, however, when you need to redirect the input and output of programs to different components of your system (e.g., printer, disk drives). For example, you might want to print (rather than view) a directory of files or send a telephone listing through a sorting program and create a new file.

- Use a DOS *redirecting* or *piping* character with a command to change the standard input and standard output of a program.
  - Redirecting symbol < directs standard input of a program (from a file).
  - Redirecting symbol > directs standard output of a program (to a file or device).
  - Piping symbol | directs the output of one program into the input of another program. On most keyboards, the pipe | character is located on the same key as the backslash (**SHIFT** ****).

- Some programs such as DIR, CHKDSK, and TREE only produce output and do not take input.

- Programs such as SORT, FIND, and MORE need input and produce output. These programs are called *filters* because they take input (such as files or programs) and change the form of the information for output.

- Not all programs can use redirection and piping.

- For DOS to find external commands such as CHKDSK, TREE, SORT, FIND, and MORE, either (1) the DOS disk containing these command files must be current when you issue the command, (2) you specify a pathname before the command verb, or (3) you first specify a PATH to these command files. To review the PATH command, see pages 19–20.

- For examples using the SORT and FIND filter programs, see pages 36–37.

Direct Input of a Program (<)

1. Type **program name < filename**
2. Press **ENTER**

Examples:

   SORT < NAMES.DOC
   FIND "201" < C:\PHONE.LST

Direct Output of a Program (>)

1. Type **program name > filename or device**
2. Press **ENTER**

Examples:

   DIR > PRN
   DATE > DATEFILE
   CHKDSK MYFILE.TXT > PRN
   DIR A:*.PIC > B:PICFILES.TXT
   TREE /F > FILES.LST
   SORT /+9 < MYFILES > PRN

Append Output to a File (>>)

This procedure appends the output of a program to the end of an existing file. If the file you specify is not present, a new file is created.

1. Type **program name >> filename**
2. Press **ENTER**

Examples:

   DIR B: >> ALLFILES.GLS
   TREE /F >> FILES.DIR
   SORT /R < DATES.LST >> EVENTS.LST

Pipe Output of One Program into Input of Another (|)

Use this command when you need to send the output of a program (program1) into a program that requires input (program 2).

1. Type **program1 | program2**
2. Press **ENTER**

Examples:

   DIR | MORE
   SORT < MYLIST | MORE
   TREE /F | FIND "BAT"

USING EDLIN LINE EDITOR

Guidelines
- DOS provides a line editor which allows you to create and edit ASCII-formatted text files.
- EDLIN is useful for creating batch files or writing short memos.
- EDLIN is an external command. You must have the EDLIN.COM file present in the current directory when you use EDLIN, you must specify its pathname when typing the command, or EDLIN.COM must be stored in a directory specified by the PATH command.

Create a File
1. From the DOS prompt, type **EDLIN newname**
2. Press **ENTER**
3. To begin inserting lines, type **I** (letter i)
4. Press **ENTER**
5. Type new line and press **ENTER**
6. Repeat Step 5 as needed
7. To finish inserting lines, press **CTRL** **BREAK** (or **CTRL** **C**)

Edit a File
1. From the DOS prompt, type **EDLIN filename**
2. If the file you are loading contains several end-of-file markers (^Z), to display the entire file, press **SPACEBAR** and type **/B**. Otherwise, only part of the file will display.
3. Press **ENTER**

Save File and Exit Edlin
1. From the asterisk prompt, type **E**
2. Press **ENTER**

Exit Edlin Without Saving File
Use this procedure to exit to the DOS prompt without saving the current edits to the displayed file.

1. From the asterisk prompt, type **Q**
2. Press **ENTER**
3. When prompted to confirm quitting, type **Y**

Display Line(s)

1. From the asterisk prompt:
   - To list the first 23 lines of file, type **L**, or
   - To list lines starting from a specific line, type **line numberL**, or
   - To list a range of lines, type **first line,last lineL**
2. Press ENTER

Examples:
25l
15,20l

Delete Line(s)

1. From the asterisk prompt:
   - To delete one line, type **line numberD**, or
   - To delete a range of lines, type **first line,last lineD**
2. Press ENTER

Examples:
14d
3,16d

Insert Line(s)

Use this command to begin typing in a new file or to add lines to an existing file. The maximum line length is 253 characters.

1. From the asterisk prompt:
   - To insert first line in a new file, type **I** (letter i), or
   - To insert a line above a specified line, type **line numberI**, or
   - To insert lines at the end of the file, type **#I**
2. Press ENTER
3. Type new line and press ENTER
4. Repeat Step 3 as needed
5. To finish inserting lines, press CTRL BREAK (or CTRL C)

Examples:
I
6I
#I

Edit a Line

This procedure displays a new line and a copy of the original line from which you can copy parts if you wish.

1. To specify line to edit, type **line number**
2. Press **ENTER**
3. To edit line, use any of these options:
   - Type new text
   - Copy one letter at a time, press **→** or **F1**
   - Delete letter to the left, press **←** or **BACKSPACE**
   - Copy up to a character, press **F2** and type **character**
   - Skip over next character, press **DEL**
   - Insert characters (on/off toggle) from cursor, press **INS**
   - Skip to a character, press **F4** and type **character**
   - Copy remaining characters in line, press **F3**
4. When finished editing line, press **ENTER**

Type Control Character

1. To type a control character, press **CTRL** **V**
2. Type desired control character in uppercase

Example: **CTRL** **V**, then **Z** (prints ^Z)

Search for Text

1. From the asterisk prompt:
   - To search for a text string in a range, type
     first line(,last line)Sstring, or
   - To search for a text string and be prompted to continue search,
     type **first line(,last line)?Sstring**
2. Press **ENTER**
3. If prompted to end search, type **Y** to end search or type **N** to continue

Examples:
10sreport
1?sAllen
15,40?sfigure

USING EDIT PROGRAM

Create or Edit ASCII File

NOTE: The Editor program uses the Editor portion of QBASIC. Make sure that QBASIC.EXE is in the DOS directory.

1. ▪ To create a file, type **EDIT newname**, or
   ▪ To edit a file, type **EDIT filename**, or
   ▪ To begin editor, type **EDIT**
2. Press `ENTER`
3. Type and edit file using keys in table
4. To print the file, press `ALT`, then type `F` `P`
5. To save changes to the file, press `ALT`, then type `F` `S`
6. To exit the editor, press `ALT`, then type `F` `X`

Cursor Movement

Move:		
	Word left/right	`CTRL` `←` / `CTRL` `→`
	Beginning/end of line	`HOME` / `END`
	Beginning of next line	`CTRL` `ENTER`
	Top/end of file	`CTRL` `HOME` / `END`

Editing Commands

Command:	Menu	`CLICK` or `ALT`
	Cancel command	`ALT` or `ESC`
Search:	Find	`CTRL` `Q` `F`
	Repeat find	`F3`
	Replace	`CTRL` `Q` `A`
Insert:	Overtype	`INS`
	Special characters	`CTRL` `P` `CTRL` *key*
Delete:	Rest of word	`CTRL` `T`
	Entire line	`CTRL` `Y`
	Rest of line	`CTRL` `Q` `Y`
Block:	Select text	`SHIFT` `↑` `↓` `←` `→`
	Erase permanently	`DEL`
	Erase leading spaces	`SHIFT` `TAB`
	Cut to Clipboard	`SHIFT` `DEL`
	Copy to Clipboard	`CTRL` `INS`
	Paste	`SHIFT` `INS`

USING DOS SHELL

Action Bar

File	Options	View	Tree	Help

Accessing/Using Commands

Access shell (use text or graphics mode) .... DOSSHELL /T or /G
Switch to/from Action bar .... **ALT** or **F10**
Move around screen .... **CLICK** or **TAB**

Choose option.................................... **CLICK** or **ENTER**
Cancel .... **CLICK** elsewhere or **ESC**
Help .... **F1** or **ALT** **H**

Exiting Dosshell

Switch to C> prompt.. **SHIFT** **F9**
   Return from C> prompt .... EXIT **ENTER**
Exit Dosshell.. **F3**

Selecting a File

Select file:
   With keyboard .... **SPACEBAR**
   With mouse .... **CLICK**
Deselect file .... **SPACEBAR**

Selecting Several Files

Select multiple files:
   With mouse .... **CTRL** **CLICK**
   Turn on ADD mode.. **SHIFT** **F8**
     and select with keyboard .... **SPACEBAR**
Select all files.......................... **CTRL** **/** or **ALT** **F** **S**
Deselect all files..................... **CTRL** **** or **ALT** **F** **L**

Running Task Swapper (Multiple Programs)

Enable task swapper....................................... **ALT** **O** **E**
Add program to list .... **SHIFT** **ENTER**
Select a program... **ALT** **TAB**
   (press **TAB** repeatedly to cycle names)
Return to shell... **CTRL** **ESC**

USING DOSKEY

Installing Doskey in Memory
Install ....DOSKEY
Install and display command history..................DOSKEY HISTORY

Displaying Commands
Previous commands...⬆ / ⬇
List commands...F7
Select command number...F9
Clear commands from buffer.................................ALT F7

Recording
Macro ....DOSKEY name=keys
    (e.g., doskey list=dir /w)
Several commands ....$T
    (e.g., doskey now=mem $tver)
Command parameters .... $1–$9
    (e.g., doskey see=dir $1)
All following parameters ....$*
    (e.g., doskey see=dir $)*

Macros
List.. DOSKEY /MACROS
Clear ....ALT F10

Cursor Movement
Beginning/end of command ....HOME / END
Previous/next word......................................CTRL ← / CTRL →

Editing
Insert/overtype ....INS
Clear line..ESC
Delete current character...DEL
Delete character left ....BACKSPACE
Delete to end of line ....CTRL END
Delete to beginning of line ....CTRL HOME
Delete to character..F4 *character*

CHANGING COUNTRY SETTINGS

Change County Settings

This example changes date and time format for the United Kingdom.

CONFIG.SYS

```
country=044,,c:\dos\country.sys
```

AUTOEXEC.BAT

```
cd \dos
keyb uk,,c:\dos\keyboard.sys
```

Change Country, Keyboard, and Code Page Settings

Use the following example to change the country settings as well as the keyboard layout, screen, and printer for Germany.

CONFIG.SYS

```
country=049,,c:\dos\country.sys
device=c:\dos\display.sys con-(ega,437,1)
device=c:\dos\printer.sys lpt1=(420,,1)
install=c:\dos\nlsfunc.exe
```

AUTOEXEC.BAT

```
mode con cp prep=((850)c:\dos\ega.cpi)
mode lpt1 cp prep=((850)c:\dos\420.cpi)
key gr,,c:\dos\keyboard.sys
chcp 850
```

View/Verify Current Code Page Settings

1. ▪ To view code page information about keyboard, monitor, and printer, type **MODE**, or
   ▪ To view code page information about one device (CON), type **MODE CON CP**, or
   ▪ To view code page information about keyboard and monitor, type **KEYB**, or
   ▪ To view active code page, type **CHCP**
2. Press **ENTER**

Quickly Switch to U.S. Keyboard

1. ▪ To switch to United States keyboard, press **CTRL** **ALT** **F1**, or
   ▪ To switch to international keyboard, press **CTRL** **ALT** **F2**

USING DIAGNOSTICS

Guidelines
- The Microsoft Diagnostics program senses your current hardware configuration and displays a wealth of technical information about your computer and how it is being used.
- Use this information to assess whether your hardware is properly configured.
- Microsoft Diagnostics displays information on:
  > Computer brand
  > Memory
  > Video
  > Network
  > Operating system
  > Mouse
  > Other adapters
  > Disk drives
  > LPT (parallel) ports
  > COM (serial) ports
  > IRQ (interrupt) status
  > Terminate-and-Stay-Resident (memory-resident) programs
  > Device drivers
- Do not run the MSD program while Windows is running. If Windows is running, exit Windows completely, then perform this procedure. If you run this program while Windows is running, the information displayed may be inaccurate.

View Diagnostic Information
1. Insert DOS disk and make that drive current
2. Type **MSD** and press `ENTER`
3. The program examines your computer and then displays information about your computer
4. To see further information on the displayed topics, `CLICK` on the topic button or press the highlighted letter of the topic button
5. To view AUTOEXEC.BAT, CONFIG.SYS, and other system files, press `ALT`, press `F`, and move highlight to desired file to view and press `ENTER`. Scroll through file with `↓` and `↑`. When finished viewing file, press `ENTER`.
6. To view memory blocks, press `ALT`, press `U`, and select `M` (Memory Block Display) or `B` (Memory Browser)
7. To exit Microsoft Diagnostics, press `ALT` `F` `X` or press `F3`

HISTORICAL LIST OF COMMANDS AND DOS VERSIONS

Versions
† 3.0–3.1 command
‡ 3.2 command
‡‡ 3.3 command
‡‡‡ 4.0 command
‡‡‡‡ 5.0 command
‡‡‡‡‡ 6.0 command
* CONFIG.SYS command

File Maintenance Commands

Change file attributes	ATTRIB †
Change directory	CHDIR or CD
Copy or append files	COPY
Delete subdirectories	DELTREE ‡‡‡‡‡
List files	DIR
Use shell interface	DOSSHELL ‡‡‡
Edit ASCII file	EDIT ‡‡‡‡
Erase files	ERASE or DEL
Copy compressed setup files	EXPAND ‡‡‡‡
Find text string	FIND
Compare files	FC ‡‡‡‡
Run program above first 64K	LOADFIX ‡‡‡‡‡
Make directory	MKDIR or MD
Display file by page	MORE
Move file/remove directory	MOVE ‡‡‡‡‡
Print ASCII file	PRINT
Recover damaged file	RECOVER
Rename a file	RENAME or REN
Selectively replace file	REPLACE †
Remove a directory	RMDIR or RD
Sort a file	SORT
List directories	TREE
Display ASCII file	TYPE
Undelete file(s)	UNDELETE ‡‡‡‡
Verify disk writing	VERIFY ON/OFF
Selectively copy files	XCOPY ‡

Disk Maintenance Commands

Reroute disk request	ASSIGN
Back up a hard disk	BACKUP
Check disk	CHKDSK
Compare sets of files	COMP
Copy files on disk	COPY *.*
Compress disk	DBLSPACE ‡‡‡‡‡
Fix fragmented disk	DEFRAG ‡‡‡‡‡
Compare two disks	DISKCOMP
Copy entire disk	DISKCOPY
Format a disk	FORMAT
Link computers from client	INTERLNK ‡‡‡‡‡
Link computers from server	INTERSVR ‡‡‡‡‡
Join drive to directory	JOIN †
Change disk label	LABEL †
Store disk information	MIRROR ‡‡‡‡
Remove viruses	MSAV ‡‡‡‡‡
Back up a hard disk	MSBACKUP ‡‡‡‡‡
View hardware information	MSD ‡‡‡‡‡
Recover damaged disk	RECOVER
Restore backed up files	RESTORE
Load file sharing	SHARE †
Substitute drive for path	SUBST †
Add system files	SYS
Unformat disk	UNFORMAT ‡‡‡‡
Display disk label	VOL
Continuously check for viruses	VSAFE ‡‡‡‡‡

Configuration Commands

Search for data files	APPEND ‡‡
Turn BREAK on/off	BREAK *
Set memory buffers	BUFFERS *
Set code page	CHCP ‡‡
Set date/time format	COUNTRY * †
Modify system date	DATE
Add device drivers	DEVICE *
Add to high memory	DEVICEHIGH * ‡‡‡‡
Load DOS into memory	DOS * ‡‡‡‡
Short help on DOS	DOSHELP ‡‡‡‡‡
Recall/edit keystrokes	DOSKEY ‡‡‡‡
Add external drive	DRIVEPARM * ↓↓↓↓
Enable expanded mem. support	EMM386 ‡‡‡‡
Store recent filenames	FASTOPEN ††
Set file control blocks	FCBS * †
Set open files	FILES *
Display help on DOS	HELP ‡‡‡‡
Load memory resident program	INSTALL †††
Load keyboard layout	KEYBxx or KEYB xx ‡‡
Set maximum drive	LASTDRIVE * †
Use high memory	LOADHIGH or LH ‡‡‡‡
Display memory usage	MEM ‡‡‡
Maximize memory	MEMMAKER ‡‡‡‡‡
Set port, monitor	MODE
Load language support	NLSFUNC ‡‡
Set NUM LOCK key	NUMLOCK * ‡‡‡‡‡
Create directory path	PATH
Conserve battery power	POWER ‡‡‡‡‡
Modify system prompt	PROMPT
Run/edit Basic program	QBASIC ‡‡‡‡
Add remark to CONFIG.SYS	REM * ‡‡‡
Select country format	SELECT †
Change environment	SET
View/set DOS version	SETVER ‡‡‡‡
Set COMMAND.COM	SHELL * or COMMAND
Create disk cache	SMARTDRV †††††
Use data stacks	STACKS * ‡‡
Change enhanced keyboard	SWITCHES * ‡‡‡
Modify system time	TIME

Commands to Avoid in Windows

You should not use the following commands while Windows is running. You can, however, use them before starting Windows.

Search for data files	APPEND
Fix fragmented disk	DEFRAG
Enable expanded mem. support	EMM386
Store recent filenames	FASTOPEN
Maximize memory	MEMMAKER
Load language support	NLSFUNC
Create disk cache	SMARTDRV
Substitute drive for path	SUBST
Continuously check for viruses	VSAFE

If running VSAFE before running Windows, add the **LOAD=C:\DOS\MWAVTSR.EXE** command to your WIN.INI file (this allows VSAFE messages to appear in Windows).

DOS COMMANDS

APPEND Specify drives/directories DOS should search for data files. DOS 3.3. See PATH. *Internal* and *External*.
  APPEND /E /X (loads APPEND capability into memory and environment)
  APPEND C:\PROGRAMS (DOS will search C:\PROGRAMS for non-executable files)
  APPEND C:\PROGRAMS;C:\ (DOS will search C:\PROGRAMS and root)
  APPEND ; (resets appended directory path)
ASSIGN Assign disk another name to reroute disk requests. *External.*
  ASSIGN (resets all drive reassignments)
  ASSIGN A=C (reroutes Drive A: requests to Drive C:)
  ASSIGN A=C B=C (reroutes Drives A: and B: requests to Drive C:)

ATTRIB Make a file ready-only, set archive attribute for BACKUP and XCOPY. *External.*
  ATTRIB B:MEMO#1 (displays attribute status of MEMO#1)
  ATTRIB +R B:MEMO#1 (makes MEMO#1 ready-only)
  ATTRIB −R B:MEMO#1 (removes read-only attribute from MEMO#1)
  ATTRIB +R C:\PERSONAL*.* (makes all files in directory read-only)
  ATTRIB +A C:\LETTER#3 (sets archive bit to allow backup, DOS 3.2)
  ATTRIB −A C:\LETTER#3 (resets archive bit to disallow backup, DOS 3.2)
  ATTRIB +A C:*.* /S (allows backup of all files on C:, DOS 3.3)
  ATTRIB +S C:\SYSTEM.TXT (makes SYSTEM.TXT a system file, DOS 5.0)
  ATTRIB −S C:\SYSTEM.TXT (removes system attribute, DOS 5.0)
  ATTRIB +H C:\NOTE.TXT (hides NOTE.TXT, DOS 5.0)
  ATTRIB −H C:\NOTE.TXT (removes hidden attribute, DOS 5.0)

BACKUP Back up files from a hard disk onto floppy disks. Not included in DOS 6.0. The Microsoft Backup program for Windows supplied with DOS 6.0 is named MWBACKUP. See MSBACKUP and RESTORE. *External.*

BACKUP C:\ A: (backs up only files in root of C: to disk in A:)

BACKUP C:\ A: /S (backs up all files in root and all directories below root)

BACKUP C:\ A: /S /D:3–14–93 (backs up files modified since date)

BACKUP C:\ A: /S /D:3–14–93 /T:15:50 (backs up after date and time, DOS 3.3)

BACKUP C:\ A: /S /M (backs up files modified since last backup)

BACKUP C:\ A: /S /M /A (adds files to existing backup disks)

BACKUP C:\BIGFILE.TXT A: (backs up single file)

BACKUP C:\ A: /S /F (Formats A: if needed, DOS 3.3. /F is not necessary in DOS 4.0)

BACKUP C:\ A: /S /L (appends date and filenames to BACKUP.LOG on root of C:, DOS 3.3)

BREAK Enable break command (`CTRL` `BREAK`) during all operations. *Internal.*

BREAK (displays break status)

BREAK ON (enables break during all operations)

BREAK OFF (enables break only during standard input/output and port operations)

CHCP Change country code page for all devices loaded in CONFIG.SYS files. You must load NLSFUNC first. Allows you to choose a code page for the current country setting loaded with COUNTRY command in CONFIG.SYS. Code page must be compatible with keyboard specified with KEYB command in CONFIG.SYS command. *Internal.*

CHCP (displays current code page, DOS 3.3)

CHCP 850 (changes current code page to 850, DOS 3.3)

CHDIR or **CD** Change current directory. *Internal.*

CD (displays current directory name)

**CD ** (changes to root directory

CD .. (changes to parent directory)

CD \CLIENT\FOLDER1\REPORT (changes to directory from root)

CD FOLDER1\REPORT (changes to directory, assuming current directory is parent to FOLDER1)

CD C:\CLIENT (makes directory current on C:, whether or not C: is the logged drive)

CHKDSK Produce a disk and memory status report, convert lost chains. *External*.

  CHKDSK (displays status of disk in default drive)

  CHKDSK C: (displays status of disk in Drive C:)

  CHKDSK C: /F (checks status and converts lost chains to files)

  CHKDSK C: /V (displays status of disk and lists directories/files)

  CHKDSK B:MYFILE.DOC (displays contiguity of MYFILE.DOC)

CLS Clear the screen. *Internal*.

  CLS (clears the screen, resets cursor to upper left)

COMMAND Invoke a secondary command processor. *Internal*.

  COMMAND (reloads command processor)

  COMMAND C: (activates COMMAND.COM again, specifies Drive C:)

  COMMAND C:\ /P (activates COMMAND.COM, permanently overwrites active command processor)

  COMMAND C:\ /C AUTOEXEC (activates COMMAND.COM, executes AUTOEXEC.BAT in the root of C:)

  COMMAND C:\ /C AUTOEXEC /E:320 (sets environment size, DOS 3.2)

  EXIT (exits active command processor to previous processor)

COMP Compare contents of two sets of files. See FC. *External*.

  COMP (prompts you for filenames to compare)

  COMP A:LETTER.TXT B:LETTER.BAK (compares the two files)

  COMP A: B: (compares files with same names and extensions in A: and B:)

  COMP A: C:\DATA (compares files with same names and extensions in A: with DATA directory of C:)

  COMP A:*.TXT A:*.BAK (compares .TXT and .BAK files with same names and different extensions)

  COMP JUNE.TXT MAY.TXT (displays comparison in hexadecimal format, DOS 5.0)

  COMP JUNE.TXT MAY.TXT /D (displays in decimal format, DOS 5.0)

  COMP JUNE.TXT MAY.TXT /A (displays differences as characters, DOS 5.0)

  COMP JUNE.TXT MAY.TXT /L (displays line numbers instead of offset, DOS 5.0)

  COMP JUNE.TXT MAY.TXT /C (ignores case, DOS 5.0)

COPY Copy or append files. Copied files replace existing files that have the same names. *Internal.*

COPY A:MEMO.TXT B: (copies file from Drive A: to Drive B:)

COPY A:MEMO.TXT C:\CLIENT1 (copies file from Drive A: to C:\CLIENT1 directory)

COPY A:MEMO.TXT C: (copies file to current directory of Drive C:)

COPY A:MEMO.TXT (copies file to current directory of Drive C:)

COPY A:MEMO.TXT A:MEMO.BAK (copies and renames file)

COPY A:MEMO.* B: (copies all files with MEMO name and different extensions—see wildcards)

COPY A:*.* B: (copies all files from Drive A: to Drive B: with the exception of hidden files, read-only files, and directories)

COPY C:\SMITH*.* A: (copies all files in SMITH directory to Drive A:

COPY FILE1+FILE2+FILE3 (appends FILES 2, 3 to end of FILE1)

COPY FILE1+FILE2 FILE3 (appends FILES 1 and 2 to FILE3, creates FILE3 if necessary)

COPY A:*.PRN A:ALLPRN.TXT (combines all .PRN files into ALLPRN.TXT file)

COPY CONFIG.SYS+CON (appends new text to the end of CONFIG.SYS)

DATE View or modify system date. See SELECT or COUNTRY command. *Internal.*

DATE (displays system's date, allows you to change it)

DATE 4/2/93 (sets system date to April 2, 1993)

DATE 4–2–93 (sets system date to April 2, 1993)

DATE 4.2.93 (sets system date to April 2, 1993)

DBLSPACE Compress hard disks and floppy disks and configures compressed disks. *External.*

DBLSPACE (The first time you type this command, it starts a setup program for compressing and configuring compressed drives, loads DBLSPACE.BIN into memory, and adds a DEVICE=DBLSPACE.SYS command to CONFIG.SYS. DOS will automatically load DBLSPACE.BIN into the top of conventional memory upon booting before the CONFIG.SYS and AUTOEXEC.BAT files execute. When you run this command subsequently, it displays compressed drives and displays a menu-driven program to work with compressed drives. DOS 6.0.)

DBLSPACE /CHKDSK /F D: (converts lost clusters to files, fixes cross-linked files, and checks validity of compressed Drive D: structure, DOS 6.0)

DBLSPACE /COMPRESS D: (Compresses files on D: (hard, floppy, or removable drive), leaves free space uncompressed and named as Drive I:. Leaves 2 megabytes uncompressed (the default). Hard disk must have 1 MB free and floppy disk must have 200K free in order to compress. DOS 6.0.)

DBLSPACE /COMPRESS D: /RESERVE=5 (Compresses as described above, but reserves 5 megabytes as uncompressed within the drive. This is useful for files that must not be compressed such as a Windows swapfile. DOS 6.0.)

DBLSPACE /CONVSTAC=vol D: (converts Stacker volume file on D: to DoubleSpace format, DOS 6.0)

DBLSPACE /CREATE C: (creates new compressed drive from free space on uncompressed Drive C: and reserves 1 megabyte of free space (the default) on C:, DOS 6.0)

DBLSPACE /CREATE C: /RESERVE=0 (creates new compressed drive from free space on uncompressed Drive C: and reserves 0 megabytes of free space on C:, DOS 6.0)

DBLSPACE /CREATE C: /SIZE=20 (creates new compressed drive allocated from 20 megabytes of free space on the uncompressed Drive C:, DOS 6.0)

DBLSPACE /DEFRAGMENT D: (Defragments compressed Drive D: to consolidate its free space. This is useful if you intend to reduce the drive size because the more consolidated free space, the smaller the drive can be reduced. DOS 6.0.)

DBLSPACE /DELETE D: (Deletes compressed Drive D:, the compressed volume file, and all files contained in the drive. You cannot delete Drive C:. To restore a deleted drive, UNDELETE the DBLSPACE.xxx compressed volume file and then mount it (see below). DOS 6.0.)

DBLSPACE /FORMAT D: (Formats compressed Drive D: and erases all files in it. You cannot format Drive C: with DBLSPACE. You cannot unformat the drive. DOS 6.0.)

DBLSPACE /INFO C: (Displays free and used space on compressed Drive C:, the name of the compression volume file, and its actual and estimated compression ratios. The /INFO switch is optional. DOS 6.0.)

DBLSPACE /LIST (lists all compressed and non-compressed drives except network drives, DOS 6.0)

DBLSPACE /MOUNT A: (assigns drive letter A: to compressed volume file (named DBLSPACE.000) so you can use files that it contains, necessary only if you unmounted a compressed volume file or wish to use a compressed floppy disk, DOS 6.0)

DBLSPACE /MOUNT=001 D: (mounts compressed volume file DBLSPACE.001 and names it Drive D:, DOS 6.0)

DBLSPACE /UNMOUNT A: (Removes connection between a mounted compressed volume file and its drive letter (A:). You cannot unmount Drive C:. DOS 6.0.)

DBLSPACE /RATIO /ALL (Changes estimated compression ratio of each compressed drive to the actual average compression ratio of the drive. DoubleSpace uses the estimated ratio of a drive to determine how much free space exists on the drive. This command does not recompress the drives. When you start the computer, DoubleSpace adjusts the estimated compression ratio to match the actual average compression ratio of all drives automatically. Use this command after storing new files on a drive or drives, thus changing the actual ratio. DOS 6.0.)

DBLSPACE /RATIO=4 D: (changes estimated compression ratio of Drive D: to 4 to 1 (range = 1.0 through 16.0 to 1), DOS 6.0)

DBLSPACE /SIZE=25 C: (Reduces or enlarges the amount of space the compressed Drive C: takes up on its uncompressed host drive to 25 megabytes. This is useful to create more free space on a host drive (containing the compressed drive) or to create more free space on the compressed drive. DOS 6.0.)

DBLSPACE /SIZE /RESERVE=10 E: (resizes compressed Drive E: so that its uncompressed host drive contains 10 megabytes of free disk space, DOS 6.0)

DBLSPACE /SIZE D: (reduces size of compressed Drive D: to as small as possible, DOS 6.0)

DEVICE=\DOS\DBLSPACE.SYS /MOVE (in CONFIG.SYS file, moves DBLSPACE.BIN from top to bottom of conventional memory (useful if other programs need access to the top of conventional memory), DOS 6.0)

DEVICEHIGH=\DBLSPACE.SYS /MOVE (In CONFIG.SYS file, moves DBLSPACE.BIN from conventional to upper memory area, if available. If not available, moves to bottom of conventional memory. DOS 6.0.)

DEFRAG Reorganize disk so that all files and free space are consolidated. This speeds up disk performance. Do not run this command under Windows. *External.*

DEFRAG C: (displays menu-driven program to defragment Drive C:, DOS 6.0)

DEFRAG C: /F (defragments Drive C: and removes any free space between files, DOS 6.0)

DEFRAG C: /U (Defragments Drive C: and leaves free space, if there is any, between files. Although this is a faster method than with /F, less free space is consolidated. You cannot use the /S (sort) switch with the /U switch. DOS 6.0.)

DEFRAG C: /F /SD /V /B /SKIPHIGH /H (defragments without free space between files, sorts files by earliest date first within directories (or N (name) E (extension) S (size) or N– E– S– D– for reverse order), verifies that moved files can be read, reboots computer upon completion, loads DEFRAG into conventional memory rather than upper memory, and moves hidden files, DOS 6.0)

DEL See ERASE. *Internal.*

DELTREE Deletes all files in directory and removes directory and all directories and their files within that directory. *External.*

    DELTREE C:\GAMES (deletes all files in C:\GAMES directory and all directories and their files within that directory, DOS 6.0)

    DELTREE C:\GAMES /Y (same as above without first prompting you to confirm deletion, DOS 6.0)

DIR List files and directories in specified directory. *Internal.*

    DIR (lists files in current drive and directory)

    DIR A: (lists files in current directory of Drive A:)

    DIR C:\DOS (lists files in \DOS directory of Drive C:)

    DIR *.DOC (lists only .DOC files in current directory)

    DIR /P (lists all files in page by page format)

    DIR /W (lists all files in wide screen format)

DIR /S (lists files in current directory and its subdirectories, DOS 5.0)

DIR /B (lists bare filename.ext format with no header or summary, DOS 5.0)

DIR /L (lists filenames in lower case, DOS 5.0)

DIR /A (lists all files including hidden and system files, DOS 5.0)

DIR /AD (lists only directory names, DOS 5.0)

DIR /AH (lists only files with hidden attribute, DOS 5.0)

DIR /AS (lists only files with system attribute, DOS 5.0)

DIR /AR (lists only files with read-only attribute, DOS 5.0)

DIR /AA (lists only files ready for archiving (backing up), DOS 5.0)

DIR /AHS (lists files that are both hidden and system, DOS 5.0)

DIR /A–D (lists files but not directories (– means "not"), DOS 5.0)

DIR /O (sorts files by directory and name (alphabetically), DOS 5.0)

DIR /ON (sorts files by name (alphabetically), DOS 5.0)

DIR /OE (sorts files by extension (alphabetically), DOS 5.0)

DIR /OG (sorts directory groups first, DOS 5.0)

DIR /OS (sorts files by size (smallest first), DOS 5.0)

DIR /OC (sorts files by compression ratio (lowest first), DOS 6.0)

DIR /OD (sorts files by date and time (earliest first), DOS 5.0)

DIR /O–S (sorts largest files first (– means "reverse"), DOS 5.0)

DIR /O–D (sorts latest files first, DOS 5.0)

DIR /OGEN (lists directories, then files by extension and by name within extension, DOS 5.0)

DIR *.WP /W /O /S /P (lists all files with combination of arguments)

DIR B: > PRN (prints list of all files on Drive B:)

DIR B: /B /L > DIRLIST (creates file with filenames)

SET DIRCMD=/P /A /OGEN (presets DIR filename and switches, DOS 5.0)

SET DIRCMD= (resets DIR filename and switches to default, DOS 5.0)

DIR /–P (overrides present switch /P, DOS 5.0)

DISKCOMP Compare contents of two floppy disks, track for track. Prompts you when to insert source and target disks. *External.*

    DISKCOMP (assumes same (default) drive for compare, prompts to replace disk)

    DISKCOMP A: B: (compares disk in A: with disk in B:)

DISKCOPY Copy entire floppy disk, track for track, including hidden files, read-only files, and directories. Formats if needed. Prompts you when to insert disks. *External.*

    DISKCOPY (copies disks in default drive)

    DISKCOPY A: (copies disk in Drive A: to default drive)

    DISKCOPY A: A: (copies disks in a single drive)

    DISKCOPY A: B: (copies disk in Drive A: to disk in Drive B:)

DOSHELP Display help information on DOS commands. Formerly HELP in DOS 5.0. Also see HELP. *External.*

    DOSHELP (displays one-line description on all DOS commands, DOS 6.0)

    DOSHELP DIR (displays help on all parameters and switches of DIR and other commands, DOS 6.0)

    DIR /? (/? displays help on all parameters and switches of any command, DOS 6.0)

DOSKEY Memory resident utility to reissue commands, edit commands, and assign macros to commands. *External.*

    DOSKEY (installs Doskey in memory to reissue commands, DOS 5.0)

    DOSKEY /INSERT (installs in insert mode, DOS 5.0)

    DOSKEY /OVERSTRIKE (installs in overtype mode, DOS 5.0)

    DOSKEY /MACROS (displays existing macros, DOS 5.0)

    DOSKEY /HISTORY (displays previous commands, DOS 5.0)

DOSKEY /REINSTALL (installs again, clears existing buffer, DOS 5.0)

DOSKEY /BUFSIZE=256 (creates smaller memory buffer, DOS 5.0)

DOSKEY SEE=DIR /W (creates macro SEE, which, when typed, performs DIR /W command, DOS 5.0)

DOSKEY SEE=DIR $1 (substitutes parameters typed after SEE to $1, $1–$9 available, DOS 5.0)

DOSKEY SEE=DIR $* (substitutes all characters typed after SEE to $*, DOS 5.0)

DOSKEY SEE= (clears macro for SEE, DOS 5.0)

DOSKEY REVIEW=MEM $TVER ($T separates commands, no space necessary after $T, DOS 5.0)

DOSSHELL Run user interface. *External.*

DOSSHELL (starts DOS shell program in same text or graphics mode as when you last ran DOSSHELL, DOS 4.0)

DOSSHELL /T (starts shell in text mode DOS 5.0)

DOSSHELL /G (starts shell in graphics mode, DOS 5.0)

DOSSHELL /B (starts shell in black and white colors, DOS 5.0)

DOSSHELL /T:RESx (sets resolution (x=L, M, or H), DOS 5.0)

DOSSHELL /G:RESx (sets resolution (x=L, M, or H), DOS 5.0)

EDIT Edit an ASCII file. QBASIC.EXE must be in same directory or path for editor to work. *External.*

EDIT (begins editor, you can open a file from within editor, DOS 5.0)

EDIT C:\CONFIG.SYS (allows you to edit CONFIG.SYS, DOS 5.0)

EDIT C:\CONFIG.SYS /B (edits in black and white, DOS 5.0)

EDIT C:\CONFIG.SYS /G (speeds CGA screen, DOS 5.0)

EDIT C:\CONFIG.SYS /H (displays maximum lines for monitor, DOS 5.0)

EDIT C:\CONFIG.SYS /NOHI (edits in 8 colors rather than 16, DOS 5.0)

EMM386 Enable or disable expanded memory support. Before you can use this command, you must load EMM386.EXE into memory using the DEVICE=EMM386 command in CONFIG.SYS. Requires 80386 computer. *External.*

EMM386 (displays status of expanded memory support, DOS 5.0)

EMM386 OFF (suspends expanded memory support, available only if handle 0 is the only handle allocated and EMM386.EXE is not accessing upper memory area, DOS 5.0)

EMM386 ON (the default — reactivates expanded memory support after it has been suspended, DOS 5.0)

EMM386 AUTO (activates EMM386.EXE only when a program calls for it, DOS 5.0)

EMM386 W=ON (enables Weitek coprocessor support if EMM386 is not suspended, high memory area is available, and DOS in not loaded into high memory, DOS 5.0)

EMM386 W=OFF (the default — disables Weitek coprocessor support, DOS 5.0)

ERASE or **DEL** Erase files. *Internal.*

DEL A:CHAP16.DOC (erases file named CHAP16.DOC on Drive A:)

DEL C:\REPORTS*.* (erases all files in REPORTS directory, prompted to confirm)

DEL C:\REPORTS (erases all files in REPORTS directory, prompted to confirm)

DEL A:*.* (erases all files on Drive A:, prompted to confirm)

DEL A:*.* /P (prompts to delete file by file, DOS 4.0)

EXIT Quit COMMAND.COM shell to previous shell. See COMMAND. *Internal.*

EXIT (leaves current command processor for previous processor)

EXPAND Expand compressed file(s) on DOS installation or update disk. *External.*

EXPAND A:SORT.EX_ C:\DOS\SORT.EXE (expands single file, DOS 5.0)

EXPAND A:*.* C:\DOS (expands all files on Drive A: to Drive C:, DOS 5.0)

FASTOPEN Store most recently accessed directories and files in memory for quicker access. See PATH. *External.*

FASTOPEN C:=100 (remembers up to 100 directories and filenames)

FASTOPEN C: /X (remembers name in expanded memory buffers, DOS 4.0)

FASTOPEN C:=100 D:=100 (remembers directories and files on several drives, DOS 4.01)

INSTALL=FASTOPEN C:=100 D:=100 (loads FASTOPEN from CONFIG.SYS, DOS 4.01)

FC Compare two files of different sizes. See COMP. *External.*

FC JUNE.TXT MAY.TXT (compares two files in ASCII mode, DOS 4.01)

FC /A JUNE.TXT MAY.TXT (compares two files in ASCII mode in abbreviated form, DOS 4.01)

FC /B SALES.PRN SALES.OLD (compares in binary mode, DOS 4.01)

FC /L SALES.PRN SALES.OLD (compares in ASCII mode even if . EXE, .COM, .SYS, .OBJ, .LIB, or .BIN, DOS 4.01)

FC /C SALES.PRN SALES.OLD (ignores case, DOS 4.01)

FC /N SALES.PRN SALES.OLD (numbers lines, DOS 4.01)

FC *.TXT NEW.TXT (compares every .TXT file against NEW.TXT, DOS 4.01)

FC A:NEW.TXT B:*.TXT (compares NEW.TXT on Drive A: with NEW.TXT on B:, DOS 4.01)

FC A:*.BAT B:*.BAT (compares every file on Drive A: with every file on B: with the same name, DOS 4.01)

FIND Find a text string within an ASCII file or list of ASCII files. *External.*

FIND "60201" LIST1 LIST2 (displays all lines with 60201 in files LIST1 and LIST2)

FIND /V "Ms" PHONE.TBL (displays all lines not containing Ms)

FIND /C "Ms" PHONE.TBL (counts all lines containing Ms)

FIND /N "Ms" PHONE.TBL (displays lines/line numbers with Ms)

FIND /I "pcx" PICS.TXT (finds pcx regardless of case, DOS 5.0)

FOR Repeat command for a specified list of files. *Internal.*

FOR %P IN (C:\DOS*.TXT) DO TYPE %P > PRN (prints all C:\DOS*.TXT files)

FOR %Z IN (???1992.* ???1993.*) DO COPY %Z A: (copies all ???1992.* and ???1993.* files in current directory to A:\)

FORMAT Format (erase) a floppy or hard disk. Check for bad sectors. *External.*

FORMAT A: (formats floppy disk in Drive A:)

FORMAT C: (formats hard disk in Drive C:)

FORMAT B: /S (formats disk in Drive B: and adds boot files)

FORMAT B: /V (formats and adds name to disk in Drive B:)

FORMAT B: /V:LETTERS (formats and names disk, DOS 4.0)

FORMAT A: /F:720 (/F sets size regardless of drive, DOS 4.0)

FORMAT A: /4 (formats double-sided low-capacity 5¼ inch (360 KB) floppy disk in high-capacity drive (Drive A:))

FORMAT A: /N:9 /T:80 (formats low-capacity 3½ inch (720 KB) disk in 1.44 MB drive)

FORMAT A: /Q (formats quickly, DOS 5.0)

FORMAT A: /F:size (size—160, 180, 320, 360, 720, 1.2, 1.44, 2.88, DOS 5.0)

FORMAT A: /U (formats unconditionally, erases all files, DOS 5.0)

HELP Display extensive help information on DOS commands. The DOS 5.0 HELP command is called DOSHELP in DOS 6.0. Displays more information than DOSHELP command. *External.*

    HELP (displays menu-driven program for finding and reviewing syntax, notes, and examples on all DOS commands, DOS 6.0)

    HELP DIR (displays help on syntax, notes, and examples of DIR and other commands, DOS 6.0)

INTERLNK Link two computers to share files. Issue this command on the client computer *after* issuing the INTERSVR command on the server computer. Client computer must load INTERLNK.EXE file in CONFIG.SYS file first (e.g., DEVICE=\DOS\INTERLNK.EXE /COM:2, see page 70 for options). DOS 6.0. *External.*

    INTERLNK (starts connection if server is ready, also displays link status, DOS 6.0)

    INTERLNK D=C (starts connection if server is ready, links client's Drive D: requests to server's Drive C:, and directs all requests for drives beyond Drive D (e.g., E, F, G) to access subsequent drives on server (e.g., D, E, F), DOS 6.0)

    INTERLNK D= (cancels redirection of client's Drive D: requests, DOS 6.0)

INTERSVR Link two computers to share files. Issue this command on the server computer *before* issuing INTERLNK command on the client computer. *External.*

    INTERSVR (starts InterInk which scans all ports for a client and allows all drives to be accessed by client in sequential order, DOS 6.0)

    INTERSVR /LPT (InterInk scans all parallel ports for client, DOS 6.0)

    INTERSVR /COM (InterInk scans all serial ports for client, DOS 6.0)

    INTERSVR /LPT:3 (InterInk transfers files through the third parallel port, DOS 6.0)

    INTERSVR /COM:2 (InterInk transfers files through the second serial port, DOS 6.0)

    INTERSVR /COM:3F8 (InterInk transfers files through a non-standard serial port where 3F8 is the port address, DOS 6.0)

    INTERSVR C: A: B: (starts InterInk and changes sequential order so that the client's first drive request accesses server Drive C:; the next drive in sequence accesses Drive A; and the next, Drive B:, DOS 6.0)

    INTERSVR /X=E: (starts InterInk and specifies that Drive E cannot be accessed by client, DOS 6.0)

    INTERSVR /B (displays screen in black and white, DOS 6.0)

INTERSVR /V (prevents conflict with computer's timer — add this switch if server stops running when you access a drive or printer through InterInk, DOS 6.0)

JOIN Join a drive to an empty directory. Useful for mounting a floppy disk onto a hard disk. Neither drives nor the directory can be current when typing JOIN command. Refer to directory (not drive) in commands. See SUBST command. *External.*

  JOIN (displays joined drives/directories)

  JOIN B: C:\BFILES (joins Drive B: to C:\BFILES directory)

  JOIN B: /D (disconnects Drive B: from directory, neither can be current)

KEYBxx Load keyboard layout. *External.*

  KEYBUK (loads United Kingdom keyboard layout)

  KEYB UK (DOS 3.3 syntax for KEYB command)

  KEYB UK,850,C:\DOS\KEYBOARD.SYS /ID:166 (uses country, code page, keyboard definition, and keyboard type parameters, DOS 4.0)

  INSTALL=C:\DOS\KEYB.COM UK (loads KEYB from CONFIG.SYS, DOS 4.0)

  INSTALL=C:\DOS\KEYB.COM UK,437,C:\DOS\KEYBOARD.SYS /ID:168 (uses parameters, DOS 4.0)

  KEYB (view current configuration)

  CTRL **ALT** **F1** (switches back to US keyboard)

  CTRL **ALT** **F2** (switches back to selected keyboard)

LABEL Change disk volume label. *External.*

  LABEL (changes label on default drive, prompts you for label)

  LABEL B: (changes label on Drive B:, prompts you for label)

  LABEL B:DISK THREE (changes label of disk in Drive B: to "DISK THREE")

LH or **LOADHIGH** Load program into upper memory area created by HIMEM.SYS and EMM386.EXE. *Internal.*

  LH C:\DOS\FASTOPEN C:=40 (loads FASTOPEN into upper memory, DOS 5.0)

  LOADHIGH C:\DOS\FASTOPEN C:=40 (loads into upper memory, DOS 5.0)

  LOADHIGH /L:0;1,42384 /S C:\DOS\SMARTDRV.EXE (loads SMARTDRV.EXE in specific location, DOS 6.0)

LOADFIX Run a program by placing above the first 64K of conventional memory. This avoids the "Packed file corrupt" message some programs receive when loaded and when you have some device drivers loaded into the upper memory area. *External.*

LOADFIX C:\WORDS\BUSCARD.EXE (runs BUSCARD application above 64K, DOS 5.0)

MEM Display memory usage. DOS 4.0. *External.*

MEM (displays used and free memory amounts)

MEM /P (displays programs in memory)

MEM /D (displays programs and internal drivers)

MEM /C (displays programs in conventional and upper memory)

MEM /M WP.EXE (displays how WP.EXE is using memory, DOS 6.0)

MEM /F (displays free areas of conventional and upper memory, DOS 6.0)

MEM /C /P (combine /P with either /D, /C, /M, or /F)

MEMMAKER Move device drivers and memory-resident programs to upper memory area. This leaves more room in conventional memory to load more programs at once and to help programs run faster. MemMaker changes your CONFIG.SYS, AUTOEXEC.BAT, and possibly SYSTEM.INI files with .UMB extensions. You can restore these files with the /UNDO switch. Re-run MemMaker whenever you add or remove a memory-resident (TSR) program or device driver. Only works on 386 computers and higher with extended memory. MemMaker requires that the program SIZER.EXE is in the same directory as MEMMAKER.EXE. Do not run this command from within Windows. *External.*

MEMMAKER (runs menu-driven program to load device drivers and memory-resident programs into upper memory area, DOS 6.0)

MEMMAKER /B (displays program in black and white, DOS 6.0)

MEMMAKER /BATCH (Runs from command line without menu-driven program. Uses all default settings. DOS 6.0.)

MEMMAKER /BATCH /T (disables IBM Token-Ring network detection, useful if such a network gives MemMaker problems, DOS 6.0)

MEMMAKER /BATCH /W0,0 (prevents MemMaker from reserving two locations in upper memory area for Windows translation buffers (default = 12,12), DOS 6.0)

MEMMAKER /SWAP:D (Specifies the current letter of your startup drive is D: in case the drive letter has changed since startup. This may be necessary if you use certain disk compression programs that swap disks. Not necessary to use this switch if you use Stacker 2.0, SuperStor, or Microsoft DoubleSpace. DOS 6.0.)

MEMMAKER /UNDO (restores CONFIG.SYS, AUTOEXEC.BAT, and WIN.INI files to the state previous to the last changes you made with MemMaker, DOS 6.0)

MKDIR or **MD** Make (create) a directory. *Internal.*

MD MYDATA (creates directory named MYDATA under current directory)

MD C:\PERSONAL\MYDATA (creates directory named MYDATA under PERSONAL)

MIRROR Record file allocation table and root directory, track file deletions, and/or record disk partition information. Use UNDELETE and UNFORMAT commands to restore erased, formatted, or damaged disks using mirror files. DOS 5.0 only; this command not included in later versions of DOS. See UNDELETE and UNFORMAT. *External.*

MIRROR (store information about the disk in the current drive, used by UNFORMAT command, DOS 5.0)

MIRROR C: (stores information about Drive C:, used by UNFORMAT command, DOS 5.0)

MIRROR A: C: D: (stores information about A:, C:, and D: in their respective root directories, DOS 5.0)

MIRROR C: /1 (stores information, erases backup copy, DOS 5.0)

MIRROR C: /TC (loads deletion-tracking for Drive C: into memory, stores deleted filenames in PCTRACKR.DEL that is used by UNDELETE command, DOS 5.0)

MIRROR C: /TC–500 /TD (loads deletion-tracking with up to 500 deletions in C: and default number of deletions in D:, DOS 5.0)

MIRROR /U (unloads deletion-tracking program from memory, DOS 5.0)

MIRROR /PARTN (stores information on how hard disk is partitioned to a file named PARTNSAV.FIL on a floppy disk, used by UNFORMAT command after hard disk is corrupted, DOS 5.0)

MODE Set printer, serial ports, modify monitor defaults. *External.*

    MODE COM1:24,N,8,1,P (sets serial port communications protocol for printing)

    MODE COM1:24,N,8,1 (sets serial port communications protocol for communicating)

    MODE LPT2:132,8,P (sets parallel port for 132 columns, 8 lines/inch, retries continuously)

    MODE LPT1=COM1 (redirects printing through serial port)

    MODE CO80 (sets color 80-character display)

    MODE CON CP PREP=((852 850)C:\DOS\EGA.CPI) (loads code pages 852 and 850 for EGA or VGA screen and keyboard; must load NLSFUNC first, DOS 3.3)

    MODE LPT1 CP PREP=((852 850)C:\DOS\4201.CPI) (loads code pages for 4201 printer, must load NLSFUNC first, DOS 3.3)

    MODE CON CP SELECT=850 (activates code page 850 for screen and keyboard; must use above PREP command first; code page must be compatible with KEYB command, DOS 3.3)

    MODE (displays current status of all devices, DOS 4.0)

MORE Display output of command by screenful. *External.*

    MORE < B:DATAFILE (displays DATAFILE by screenful)

    DIR | MORE (displays list of files by screenful)

MOVE Move files or rename directory. Moved files replace existing files that have the same names. A destination is always required. *External.*

    MOVE A:SALES93.DOC B: (moves file from Drive A: to Drive B:, DOS 6.0)

    MOVE A:SALES93.DOC C:\SMITH (moves file from Drive A: to C:\SMITH directory, DOS 6.0)

    MOVE A:SALES93.DOC C: (moves file to current directory of Drive C:, DOS 6.0)

    MOVE A:SALES93.DOC . (moves file to current directory of the logged drive, DOS 6.0)

    MOVE \OLD\NOTES.WP . (moves file to current directory of the logged drive, DOS 6.0)

    MOVE NOTES.WP C:\WP\FILES (moves file from current directory to C:\WP\FILES\ directory, DOS 6.0)

    MOVE A:*.* B: (moves all files from Drive A: to B:, DOS 6.0)

    MOVE A:MEMO*.* B: (moves all files with MEMO name and different extensions—see WILDCARDS, DOS 6.0)

    MOVE C:\SMITH*.* A: (moves all files in SMITH directory to Drive A:, DOS 6.0)

MOVE A:MEMO.TXT B:MEMO.BAK (Moves file and renames it. You can only rename one file at a time (no wildcards). DOS 6.0.)

MOVE C:\DATABASE C:\DATA (Renames directory from C:\DATABASE to C:\DATA. You cannot move a directory to a new location on the directory tree by typing a different destination path. DOS 6.0)

MOVE BOB STEVE (renames BOB directory to STEVE in current directory, DOS 6.0)

MSAV Scan memory and specified drives on your computer for viruses. This creates a CHKLIST.MS file in each directory. CHKLIST.MS contains checksum information against which to compare subsequent scans of files. To interrupt scanning, press **ESC**. The Microsoft Anti-Virus program for Windows supplied with DOS 6.0 is named MWAV. Also see VSAFE. *External.*

MSAV (Displays graphical interface. Sets the current drive as the work drive to scan. DOS 6.0.)

MSAV C: (Displays graphical interface. Sets Drive C: as the work drive to scan. DOS 6.0.)

MSAV /A (automatically scans all drives except Drives A: and B:, DOS 6.0)

MSAV /L (automatically scans all local drives except network drives, DOS 6.0)

MSAV C: /S (automatically scans Drive C: but does not remove the viruses it finds, DOS 6.0)

MSAV C: /C (automatically scans Drive C: and removes the viruses it finds, DOS 6.0)

MSAV C: /P (automatically scans Drive C: using command-line interface instead of graphical interface, DOS 6.0)

MSAV C: /N (automatically displays a text file if it exists named MSAV.TXT in the same directory as MSAV.EXE, then scans Drive C: using command-line interface instead of graphical interface, DOS 6.0)

MSAV C: /P /F (turns off display of filenames being automatically scanned in command-line interface (/P or /N switches), DOS 6.0)

MSAV C: /R (creates a report named MSAV.RPT in the root directory of scanned Drive C:, DOS 6.0)

MSAV /VIDEO (displays available switches to change video and mouse modes, DOS 6.0)

MSBACKUP Back up one or more files from one disk to others. Restore files to the original or a different disk with this same command. The first time you run MSBACKUP, the program configures itself and tests your hardware. Replaces previous BACKUP command. *External.*

MSBACKUP (starts menu-driven program to back up or restore files using DEFAULT.SET for setup, DOS 6.0)

MSBACKUP MONTHLY (Uses MONTHLY.SET for setup to specify files to back up and the type of backup to perform,. You can create up to 50 setup files. DOS 6.0.)

MSBACKUP /BW (uses black and white screen , DOS 6.0)

MSBACKUP /LCD (sets video mode for laptop display, DOS 6.0)

MSBACKUP /MDA (uses a monochrome display adapter, DOS 6.0)

MSD Display menu-driven screens of technical information about your computer's hardware using Microsoft Diagnostics program. Read technical files such as AUTOEXEC.BAT and WIN.INI. *External.*

MSD (displays menu of technical information about processor, memory, video, network, version, mouse, adapters, drives, ports, IRQ status, memory-resident programs, and device drivers, DOS 6.0)

MSD /I (runs MSD without initially detecting hardware, in case you cannot start MSD, DOS 6.0)

MSD /B (runs MSD in black and white, DOS 6.0)

MSD /F C:\INFO.TXT (prompts you for name, address, phone number, and comments, then creates complete report in a file you specify - INFO.TXT, DOS 6.0)

MSD /P C:\INFO.TXT (same as above without prompting you for information, DOS 6.0)

MSD /S (displays report to the screen without prompting you for information, DOS 6.0)

NLSFUNC Load national language support to allow you to change country code or code page without rebooting. Also allows you to change code page for all devices at one time. Use with COUNTRY= in CONFIG.SYS, CHCP, and MODE commands. Load DISPLAY.SYS and/or PRINTER.SYS devices first. *External.*

NLSFUNC (loads default COUNTRY.SYS in specified or root directory, DOS 3.3)

NLSFUNC NEWCODE.SYS (loads country-specific information, DOS 3.3)

INSTALL=C:\DOS\NLSFUNC.EXE C:\DOS\COUNTRY.SYS
(locates COUNTRY.SYS if COUNTRY= is not in CONFIG.SYS file, DOS 3.3)

PATH Specify which drives and directories DOS should search for executable files. *Internal.*
PATH (displays current path)
PATH C:\;C:\WORD;C:\SHEET;..;C:.;C:\DOS (sets new path)
PATH ; (resets directory path)

POWER Conserve power when programs and hardware are idle. This is useful for battery-operated computers such as laptops. POWER.EXE must be installed via the CONFIG.SYS file first (e.g., DEVICE=C:\DOS\POWER.EXE ADV (see other switches below)). *External.*
POWER (displays current power setting, DOS 6.0)
POWER ADV (conserves power when programs and hardware are idle, same as ADV:REG, DOS 6.0)
POWER ADV:MAX (maximum power conservation, DOS 6.0)
POWER ADV:REG (balances power conservation with program and hardware performance, DOS 6.0)
POWER ADV:MIN (least amount of conservation - use if programs or hardware performance is not satisfactory, DOS 6.0)

POWER STD (if your computer has Advanced Power Management, STD uses your computer's power management; otherwise, turns off power management, DOS 6.0)
POWER OFF (turns off power management, DOS 6.0)

PRINT Print an ASCII file. *External.*
PRINT (displays print queue)
PRINT A:TOTALS (prints the file)
PRINT *.PRN (prints a group of files)
PRINT CHAP1 CHAP2 CHAP3 (prints list of files)
PRINT /C TEST.DOC (removes TEST.DOC from queue)
PRINT /T (removes all files from queue)

PROMPT Modify system (A>) prompt. *Internal.*
PROMPT (removes previous prompt, returns to normal prompt)
PROMPT PG (displays current drive and directory)

QBASIC Edit and run basic language programs. Must be in same directory as EDIT.COM for EDIT to run. *External.*
QBASIC (begins editor, you can open a file from within editor, DOS 5.0)
QBASIC CHART.BAS (edits CHART.BAS program, DOS 5.0)
QBASIC CHART (edits CHART.BAS program, DOS 5.0)
QBASIC /B CHART.BAS (edits in black and white, DOS 5.0)

QBASIC /G CHART.BAS (speeds CGA screen, DOS 5.0)
QBASIC /H CHART.BAS (displays maximum lines for monitor, DOS 5.0)
QBASIC /NOHI CHART.BAS (edits in 8 colors rather than 16, DOS 5.0)
QBASIC /RUN CHART.BAS (runs CHART.BAS program, then displays the program unless it contains SYSTEM command, DOS 5.0)
QBASIC /EDITOR (runs text editor program, DOS 5.0)

RECOVER Restore a damaged file or disk with damaged directory. *External*.
RECOVER C:\CATALOG.DOC (removes damaged sectors from file, works best on ASCII files)
RECOVER B: (recovers and renames files when directory is damaged)

RENAME or **REN** Give existing file another name. *Internal*.
REN A:REPORT REPORT#1 (renames REPORT)
REN *.TXT *.PRN (changes .TXT extensions to .PRN)

REPLACE Selectively replace files, DOS 3.2. Checks for existence before replacing. *External*.
REPLACE A:PROG1.BAS B: (replaces PROG1.BAS (if exists) on Drive B:)
REPLACE A:*.BAS B: (replaces .BAS files on Drive B:)
REPLACE A:*.BAS C:\PROGRAMS (replaces .BAS files in PROGRAMS directory)
REPLACE A:*.BAS B: /A (adds new files, does not replace existing files)
REPPLACE A:*.BAS B: /P (prompts for selective replacing)
REPLACE A:*.BAS B: /A /P (prompts for selective adding)
REPLACE A:*.BAS B: /R (allows replacing read-only files)
REPLACE A:*.BAS C:\ /S (replaces in all directories of Drive C:)
REPLACE A:*.BAS B: /W (waits to prompt user to insert disks)
REPLACE A:*.BAS B: /U (replaces with updated (newer) files only, DOS 4.0)

RESTORE Restore backed up files from floppy disk to original or different hard disk. See BACKUP. *External*.
RESTORE A: C:*.* (restores all files in root of Drive C:)
RESTORE A: C:*.* /S (restores all files and directories from root and below)
RESTORE A: C:*.* /S /P (prompts to replace with older versions of files)
RESTORE A: C:\FILES*.* (restores subdirectory)

RESTORE A: C:\FILES\JACK001.WK1 (restores single file)
RESTORE A: C:*.* /B:3–14–92 /S /P (restores files modified on or before date, DOS 3.3)
RESTORE A: C:*.* /B:3–14–92 /E:15:30 (restores files modified on or before date and time, DOS 3.3)
RESTORE A: C:*.* /A:3–14–92 (restores files modified on or after date, DOS 3.3)
RESTORE A: C:*.* /A:3–14–92 /L:15:30 (restores files modified on or after date and time, DOS 3.3)
RESTORE A: C:*.* (restores all files in root of Drive C:)
RESTORE A: C:*.* /D (lists names without restoring, DOS 5.0)

RMDIR or **RD** Remove an empty directory. *Internal.*
RD C:\MYFILES (removes MYFILES directory from root of C:)
RD C:\CLIENT1\REPORTS (removes REPORTS directory)
RD MEMOS (removes MEMOS directory under current directory)

SELECT Format new boot disk with country formatting. Copies DOS files. Creates CONFIG.SYS file with COUNTRY=xxx, AUTOEXEC.BAT file with KEYBxx. Not in DOS 5–0. *External.*
SELECT 033 FR (Formats Drive B:, adds French formatting. Drive A: is default drive. Copies DOS files from Drive A: to B:)
SELECT A: B: 033 FR (Formats Drive B:, adds French formatting. Copies DOS files to Drive B:.)
SELECT A: C: 033 FR (Formats Drive C:, adds French formatting. Copies DOS files to root of Drive C:.)
SELECT A: C:\DOSFILES 033 FR (Formats Drive C:, adds French formatting. Creates DOSFILES directory, copies DOS files to it.)

SET View or add string variables to operating system environment. *Internal.*
SET (displays current environment strings)
SET COMSPEC=C:\COMMAND.COM (set new location for COMMAND.COM)
SET COMSPEC= (removes current string for COMSPEC)

SETVER Change the DOS version reported by a program. *External.*
DEVICE=C:\SETVER.EXE (required device to run SETVER command, DOS 5.0)
SETVER (displays current version table, DOS 5.0)
SETVER C:\DOS (specifies location of SETVER.EXE, DOS 5.0)
SETVER VIEWER.EXE 5.00 (changes VIEWER.EXE to report version 5.00 to DOS, DOS 5.0)
SETVER VIEWER.EXE /DELETE (deletes VIEWER.EXE from version table, DOS 5.0)

SETVER VIEWER.EXE /DELETE /QUIET (deletes VIEWER.EXE without displaying message, DOS 5.0)

SHARE Allow file sharing. See FCBS command. *External.*
  SHARE (loads file sharing support with default settings)
  SHARE /F:3072 /L:30 (loads new amount of file space and locks)

SMARTDRV Improve speed of disk operations by creating disk cache in extended memory. Loads automatically into upper memory area, if available. Do not use this command after you start up Windows. For SMARTDRV to use extended memory, HIMEM.SYS or other LIM extended memory manager must be loaded first. SMARTDRV.EXE replaces SMARTDRV.SYS from DOS 5.0. *External.*
  C:\DOS\SMARTDRV (creates disk cache based on amount of available memory when Windows is not running, specifies location in C:\DOS, enables caching on all hard disk drives, enables read-caching (no write-caching) on floppy disk drives and Interlnk drives, but does not cache CD-ROM drives, compressed drives, or Microsoft Flash memory-card drives, DOS 6.0)
  C:\DOS\SMARTDRV 2048 1024 (creates disk cache of 2048K reducible to as small as 1024 for Windows, specifies location in C:\DOS, DOS 6.0)
  C:\DOS\SMARTDRV /L /Q (creates disk cache, /L prevents SMARTDRV from loading into upper memory area, /Q prevents SMARTDRV from displaying error and status messages at startup, DOS 6.0)
  C:\DOS\SMARTDRV /S (creates disk cache, /S displays additional status information, DOS 6.0)
  C:\DOS\SMARTDRV /E:4096 (creates disk cache, DOS 6.0)
  C:\DOS\SMARTDRV /E:4096 /B:8 (creates disk cache, /E limits the amount of cache moved at one time to 4096 bytes — default is 8192 bytes, /B sets size of read-ahead buffer to 8K (must be a multiple of /E — default is 16K bytes, DOS 6.0)
  C:\DOS\SMARTDRV /E:4096 /B:8 A- B- C+ D+ (same as above, but disables caching on Drives A: and B:, enables caching on hard disk Drive C:, and enables read-caching on Drive D: (write-cashing not available to Interlnk drives), DOS 6.0)
  SMARTDRV C+ (after disk cache is running, enables caching for Drive C:, DOS 6.0)
  SMARTDRV D– (after disk cache is running, disables caching for Drive D:, DOS 6.0)

SMARTDRV D (after disk cache is running, enables read-caching and disables write-caching to Drive D:, DOS 6.0)

SMARTDRV /C (after disk cache is running, writes all cache memory to hard disk — useful to finish all disk writing before you turn off computer , DOS 6.0)

SMARTDRV /R (after disk cache is running, clears contents of cache and restarts SMARTDRV, DOS 6.0)

DEVICE=C:\DOS\SMARTDRV.EXE /DOUBLE_BUFFER (Enables SMARTDRV to run on some computers with a SCSI device or hard drive and some ESDI or MCA devices if EMM386.EXE or Windows is running. To test if you need double buffering, add this command to CONFIG.SYS, add C:\DOS\SMARTDRV command to AUTOEXEC.BAT, reboot, run MEMMAKER, type MEM /C /P to confirm that upper memory area is in use, and type SMARTDRV to display information. If a "yes" appears under Buffering column, you need double buffering. You can use this CONFIG.SYS command together with SMARTDRV command at the command prompt or in AUTOEXEC.BAT. DOS 6.0)

SORT Sort contents of a file. *External.*

SORT < NAME.LST (sorts NAME.LST to the screen)

SORT < NAME.LST > NAME.LST (sorts and updates NAME.LST)

SORT < NAME.LST > ALPHA (sorts NAME.LST into file ALPHA)

SORT /R < NAME.LST (sorts in reverse order)

SORT /+24 < NAME.LST (sorts on the 24th column)

DIR | SORT (displays sorted list of files)

SUBST Substitute a drive name for a directory. See JOIN and LASTDRIVE commands. *External.*

SUBST (displays current substitutions)

SUBST D: C:\DBASE\FILES (allows you to refer to Drive D: for C:\DBASE\FILES directory)

SUBST D: /D (deletes substitution for Drive D:)

SYS Add operating system files to a blank or boot disk. *External.*

SYS D: (Adds operating system (boot) files to disk in Drive B:. Add (COPY) the COMMAND.COM file to make disk bootable.)

SYS A: B: (copies system files from A: to B:, DOS 4.0)

TIME View or modify system time. *Internal.*

TIME 08:15 (sets time to 8:15 AM)

TIME 08.15 (sets time to 8:15 AM)

TIME 20:15 (sets time to 8:15 PM)

TIME 08:15:20.50 (sets hours, minutes, seconds, hundredths)
TIME 8:15P (sets time to 8:15 PM, DOS 4.0)

TREE List all directories on a disk. *External.*
  TREE (lists all directory names in current drive)
  TREE C: (lists all directory names on Drive C:)
  TREE C: /F (lists all directory and file names on Drive C:)
  TREE C: /F | MORE (lists directory and file names by screenful)
  TREE /A (displays tree in ASCII | – + and \ characters, DOS 4.0)

TYPE Display contents of an ASCII file. *Internal.*
  TYPE MEMO.TXT (displays MEMO.TXT to screen)
  TYPE MEMO.TXT | MORE (displays MEMO.TXT by screenful)

UNDELETE Restore previously deleted file(s) to disk. Type this
  command from the C> prompt or add to AUTOEXEC.BAT.
  Microsoft Undelete for Windows is included in DOS 6.0. *External.*
  UNDELETE /LOAD (loads memory-resident portion of Delete
    Sentry or Delete Tracker into memory using information in
    UNDELETE.INI file, if present; otherwise, uses default settings,
    DOS 6.0)
  UNDELETE /SC (loads Delete Sentry program into memory
    using UNDELETE.INI settings, if present, and enables protection
    of Drive C: or, if UNDELETE.INI specifies drives, protects those

drives, rather than the drive specified after /S, DOS 6.0)
UNDELETE /TC–300 (loads Delete Tracker program into
  memory, creates PCTRACKER.DEL file to track up to 300 files,
  and enables deletion tracking for Drive C:, DOS 6.0)
UNDELETE /PURGEC (deletes files in SENTRY directory on
  Drive C:, DOS 6.0)
UNDELETE /U (unloads memory-resident portion of Undelete
  command from memory, disables Undelete command, DOS 6.0)
UNDELETE /STATUS (displays undelete protection in effect on
  each drive, DOS 6.0)
UNDELETE C:\ /LIST (lists all deleted files in root of C: that can
  be restored, DOS 5.0)
UNDELETE C:\LIST /DS (lists files in available to undelete using
  Delete Sentry created by UNDELETE /S command, DOS 6.0)
UNDELETE C:\ /LIST /DT (lists files in deletion-tracking file
  created by MIRROR (DOS 5.0) or UNDELETE /T (DOS 6.0)
  command, DOS 5.0)
UNDELETE C:\ /LIST /DOS (lists files that DOS recognizes as
  deleted but recoverable, DOS 5.0)
UNDELETE (undeletes all files in current directory, prompting for
  confirmation; checks Delete Sentry if present, then deletion-
  tracking file if present, otherwise DOS directory, DOS 5.0)

UNDELETE MYFILE.WP (undeletes MYFILE.WP, prompting for confirmation, DOS 5.0)

UNDELETE C:*.TXT (undeletes .TXT files in root of C:, prompting for confirmation, DOS 5.0)

UNDELETE /DT (undeletes all files in current directory in deletion-tracking file, prompting for confirmation, DOS 5.0)

UNDELETE /DOS (undeletes all files in current directory recognized by DOS, prompting for confirmation, DOS 5.0)

UNDELETE /ALL (undeletes all files in current directory without prompting; checks Delete Sentry if present, then deletion-tracking file if present, otherwise checks DOS directory and substitutes # or % for first character, DOS 5.0)

UNDELETE C:*.TXT /ALL (undeletes all .TXT files in root of C: without prompting for confirmation; checks Delete Sentry if present, then deletion-tracking file if present, otherwise checks DOS directory, DOS 5.0)

UNDELETE /ALL /DS (undeletes files in Delete Sentry without prompting, DOS 6.0)

UNDELETE /ALL /DT (undeletes files in deletion-tracking file without prompting, DOS 5.0)

UNDELETE /ALL /DOS (undeletes DOS-recognized files without prompting, DOS 5.0)

UNFORMAT Restore root directory and file allocation table of a hard disk or floppy disk that was erased by FORMAT command or restructured by RECOVER command. *External.*

UNFORMAT A: (unformats disk in Drive A:, DOS 5.0)

UNFORMAT A: /TEST (displays how UNFORMAT will recover information, DOS 5.0)

UNFORMAT A: /L (unformats A:, lists all file and directory names found, DOS 5.0)

UNFORMAT A: /P (unformats A:, prints messages to LPT1, DOS 5.0)

UNFORMAT A: /J (tests if unformat can restore disk with mirror file, does not unformat, DOS 5.0 only)

UNFORMAT A: /U (unformats A: without mirror file (cannot restore entire fragmented files), DOS 5.0 only)

UNFORMAT A: /U /L /TEST /P (unformats without mirror file, lists, tests, and prints information, DOS 5.0 only)

UNFORMAT /PARTN (prompts you to insert floppy disk with PARTNSAV.FIL created by MIRROR /PARTN command, restores partition table of corrupted disk, DOS 5.0 only)

UNFORMAT /PARTN /L (displays current partition table, does not restore, DOS 5.0 only)

VER Display version number of DOS. *Internal.*
  VER (display version of DOS)

VERIFY Have DOS check if file is readable after writing (e.g., after COPY command). *Internal.*
  VERIFY (display state of VERIFY)
  VERIFY ON (sets VERIFY on)
  VERIFY OFF (sets VERIFY off)

VOL Display disk volume label. *Internal.*
  VOL (displays label on logged drive)
  VOL C: (displays label on Drive C:)

VSAFE Continuously monitor your computer for viruses. This memory resident program requires 22K of memory. Do not type the VSAFE command while using Windows. Turn off VSAFE before running Windows installation program. If running VSAFE before running Windows, add the LOAD command described below to your WIN.INI file. Also see MSAV. *External.*
  VSAFE (Loads virus checking into memory and begins monitoring drives and memory for viruses. Press **ALT** **V** to view VSAFE screen once it is loaded into memory. You can toggle options on and off or unload VSAFE from memory. DOS 6.0.)
  VSAFE /2+ /3+ /7+ /8+ (sets all checking options that default to "off" to "on," DOS 6.0)
  VSAFE /NE (prevents VSAFE from loading into expanded memory, DOS 6.0)
  VSAFE /NX (prevents VSAFE from loading into extended memory, DOS 6.0)
  VSAFE /AM (sets hot key that activates VSAFE screen to **ALT** plus a key (**M**), (default = **ALT** **V**), DOS 6.0)
  VSAFE /CS (sets hot key that activates VSAFE screen to **CTRL** plus a key (**S**), DOS 6.0)
  VSAFE /N (monitors network drives as well, DOS 6.0)
  VSAFE /D (turns off checksumming, DOS 6.0)
  VSAFE /U (unloads VSAFE from memory, DOS 6.0)
  LOAD=C:\DOS\MWAVTSR.EXE (Add this command to WIN.INI if you intend to use Windows after VSAFE is started. This command allows VSAFE messages to appear in Windows. DOS 6.0.)

XCOPY Copy directories, selectively copy files, DOS 3.2. *External.*
  XCOPY C:\ D: (copies all files in root of Drive C: to root of Drive D:)
  XCOPY C:\ D:\ /S (copies all files in root and below, creates subdirectories)

XCOPY C:\ D:\ /S /E (copies all files in root and below, creates empty directories, if needed)

XCOPY C:\ D:\ /S /P (prompts you to confirm each file copied)

XCOPY C:\ D:\ /S /W (waits to prompt user to insert disks)

XCOPY C:\ D:\ /S /A (copies all files with archive attribute set on, does not reset archive attribute)

XCOPY C:\ D:\ /S /M (copies all files with archive attribute on, resets archive attribute)

XCOPY C:\ D:\ /S /D:3–5–92 (copies all files modified after specified date)

XCOPY C:\ D:\SMITH /S (copies all files in root and below, to SMITH directory, creates subdirectories)

XCOPY C:\MARTIN D:\ /S (copies all files in MARTIN and below to root of Drive D:)

XCOPY C:\MARTIN C:\SMITH /S (copies MARTIN directory into SMITH directory)

XCOPY C:\MYFILE.DOC D:\MYFILE.BAK (copies and renames file)

CONFIG.SYS COMMANDS

BREAK Enable break command (`CTRL` `BREAK`) during all operations.
BREAK=ON (enables break during all operations)
BREAK=OFF (enables break only during standard input/output and port operations)

BUFFERS Set number of memory buffers.
BUFFERS=15 (allows up to 15 memory buffers)
BUFFERS=15,3 (allows 3 look-ahead buffers, DOS 4.0)
BUFFERS=500,5 /X (uses expanded memory, DOS 4.0)

COUNTRY Set date/time format, currency symbol, decimal separator.
COUNTRY=044 (selects United Kingdom formatting)

DEVICE Add device drivers.
DEVICE=VDISK.SYS 200 512 64 (installs DOS virtual (RAM) disk)
DEVICE=C:\DOS\INTERLNK.EXE /COM:2 (links computers by the second serial port, loads into UMB by default)

DEVICEHIGH Load device drivers into UMA (Upper Memory Area) between 640K and 1024K.

DEVICEHIGH=/L:1,12048 C:\DOS\SETVER.EXE (loads SETVER.EXE into specific location, DOS 6.0)

DOS Load DOS partially into HMA (High Memory Area above 1024K) and/or maintain link with UMB (Upper Memory Area between 640K and 1024K). Must install HIMEM.SYS first.
DOS=HIGH (loads DOS partially into HMA (High Memory Area), DOS 5.0)
DOS=HIGH,UMB (loads DOS partially into HMA, maintains link between conventional and upper memory area, DOS 5.0)

DRIVPARM Add external floppy, hard, or tape drive.
DRIVPARM /D3 /C /F:5 (adds a hard D: drive, DOS 5.0)

FCBS Set number of file control blocks open for file sharing.
FCBS=8,4 (allows 8 files open, first 4 cannot be closed by DOS)

FILES Set the number of open files possible.
FILES=20 (allows 20 open files at one time)

INSTALL Load memory resident programs such as FASTOPEN, KEYB, NLSFUNC, SHARE.
INSTALL=C:\DOS\SHARE.EXE (loads SHARE from CONFIG.SYS, DOS 4.0)

LASTDRIVE Set last drive name allowable.
   LASTDRIVE=H (allows you to SUBST or name drives up to H)

REM Type a remark (comment) in CONFIG.SYS file. You can also use ; (semicolon) at the beginning of a remark.
   REM Following commands load devices into UMA (sample remark, DOS 4.0)
   ; Following commands load devices into UMA (same as REM)

SHELL Specify name and location of command processor.
   SHELL=COMMAND.COM C: (activates COMMAND.COM in new location)
   SHELL=COMMAND.COM C:\ /P (replaces processor in memory)
   SHELL=COMMAND.COM C:\ /E320 (sets environment size, DOS 3.2)

STACKS Allow use of data stacks for hardware interrupts.
   STACKS=9,256 (allow up to 9 stacks of 256 bytes each)

SWITCHES Force enhanced keyboard to act like standard keyboard.
   SWITCHES=/K (makes enhanced keyboard behave like standard keyboard; if using ANSI.SYS device, add /K to DEVICE=ANSI.SYS line, DOS 4.0)

Menu Commands in CONFIG.SYS (DOS 6.0)
   INCLUDE=blockname
   MENUITEM=blockname[,menutext]
   MENUDEFAULT=blockname[,timeout]
   MENUCOLOR=x[,y]
   SUBMENU=blockname[,menutext]
   NUMLOCK=ON or OFF

Device Drivers in CONFIG.SYS (DOS 6.0)
Following are device drivers that you can load into your computer's memory with either the DEVICE= or DEVICEHIGH= commands:

ANSI.SYS	**HIMEM.SYS**
CHKSTATE.SYS	**INTERLNK.EXE**
DBLSPACE.SYS	**POWER.EXE**
DISPLAY.SYS	**RAMDRIVE.SYS**
DRIVER.SYS	**SETVER.EXE**
EGA.SYS	**SMARTDRV.EXE**
EMM386.EXE	

Two files, COUNTRY.SYS and KEYBOARD.SYS are not device drivers. Do not add them to your CONFIG.SYS file.

BATCH FILE COMMANDS

@

Syntax:
   @command

Use this DOS 3.3 (and later) feature to keep the batch file command from displaying on the screen.

Examples:
   @ECHO OFF
   @CLS

CALL

Syntax:
   CALL batchfile batchparameters

Use this DOS 3.3 (and later) command to temporarily run a batch file and return to the current batch file. Example: **CALL C:\DISKNOTE**

CHOICE

Syntax:
   CHOICE /C:keys text
   CHOICE /C:keys /N /S /T:default keys,sec. text

Use this DOS 6.0 command to pause batch file and prompt user to press a specific key. Appears as such: Text [A,B,C]?. The first key has an errorlevel of 1, second is 2, etc. List IF ERRORLEVEL commands in batch file in reverse order (see example below). /N does not display key choices, just the text. /S requires the user to be case sensitive (e.g., p will not equal P). /T pauses specified seconds if there is no response and executes the default key. Text is optional. Surround text with " " if it contains a \.

Examples:
   CHOICE /C:ABC Which drive
   IF ERRORLEVEL 3 GOTO DRIVEC
   IF ERRORLEVEL 2 GOTO DRIVEB
   IF ERRORLEVEL 1 GOTO DRIVEA
   CHOICE /C:YNC /N Yes, No, or Continue?
   CHOICE Do you want to continue (no /C defaults to YN)

ECHO

Syntax:
ECHO OFF
ECHO ON
ECHO statement
ECHO

Use the ECHO OFF command to hide the display of batch file commands (including REM statements) as they are being issued. To display a remark while ECHO is OFF, type ECHO *statement* (up to 12 characters). When DOS closes a batch file, ECHO ON will resume. To view if ECHO is currently on or off, type ECHO by itself.

Examples:
ECHO OFF
ECHO ON
ECHO Now place second disk in Drive A:
ECHO
@ECHO OFF (@ keeps from displaying, DOS 3.3)

FOR..IN..DO

Syntax:
FOR %%any letter IN (file list) DO command

Use this command to repeat a DOS command or batch file subcommand for a specified list of files (may include wildcards but not pathnames). DOS substitutes each file you list into the %%letter variable name. Use the variable name as a variable in the command.

Examples:
FOR %%X IN (A:*.*) DO IF %%X==%1 ECHO %%X Found in A:! (When user executes batch file with a filename as the first parameter, this command searches in A: for that file.)
FOR %%Q IN (*.WK1 *.DOC *.DBF) DO COPY %%Q B: (copies all .WK1, .DOC, and .DBF files in current directory to B:)

GOTO

Syntax:

> GOTO label

Use this command along with a **:label** marker to create a programming loop. **:label** must appear at the beginning of a line (only the first 8 characters are significant). When your batch file reaches the GOTO command, it will jump forward or backward to the line following the **:label**.

Example batch file:

```
ECHO OFF
IF %1==50 GOTO LOOP1
GOTO END
:LOOP1
ECHO You chose 50!
:END
```

IF

Syntax:

> IF condition command
> IF NOT condition command

Use this programming command to test one of three types of conditions:

1. **ERRORLEVEL number** (True if previous program had an exit decimal number of *number* or higher.)
2. **string1==string 2** (True if both character strings are identical, including upper and lower case.)
3. **EXIST filename** (True if filename is present, pathnames not allowed.)

Examples:

```
IF ERRORLEVEL 1 ECHO Check program and retry.
IF %1==Patty GOTO PATTY
FOR %%Y IN (A:*.*) DO IF NOT %1==%%Y COPY %%Y C:
IF EXIST %2 ERASE %2
```

PAUSE

Syntax:
PAUSE message

Use this command to temporarily stop the batch file until the user presses a key. If the user presses `CTRL` `BREAK` (or `CTRL` `C`), the batch file will terminate processing. The optional message of up to 121 characters will display on the screen if ECHO is ON. The message "Strike a key when ready...." always appears whenever a PAUSE command is issued.

Examples:
PAUSE
PAUSE Place program disk in Drive A:

REM

Syntax:
REM message

Use this command as a programming note to yourself if ECHO is OFF or to display a message to the user if ECHO is ON. You can type an optional message up to 123 characters long. The message must immediately follow the REM command.

Example:
REM This program checks for disk errors.

SHIFT

Syntax:
SHIFT

Use this procedure when a user enters more than 9 parameters. Every time you issue the SHIFT command, the parameters shift to a lower number (e.g., parameter %10 becomes parameter %9).

Example: **SHIFT**

CHECKLIST OF IMPORTANT COMMANDS

☑ **Change Logged Drive (A:)**

1. At the operating system prompt, type the drive letter (e.g., A, B, C), **:** (colon), and press **ENTER**
2. The operating system prompt will display the new logged drive (e.g., A>, B>, C>)

Examples:

C>**A:** (Displays A> prompt.)
A>**B:** (Displays B> prompt.)
A>**C:** (Displays C> prompt.)

☑ **Change Current Directory (CD)**

1. ▪ To view the name of the current directory, type **CD**
   ▪ To change to the root directory, type **CD **
   ▪ To change to a subdirectory, type **CD** and press **SPACEBAR** Type the path of subdirectories from the root directory to the directory you wish (separate each subdirectory with a \\).
2. Press **ENTER**

Examples:

C>**CD**
C>**CD **
C>**CD \\WORD\\LETTERS**

NOTE: Omitting the first \\ (backslash) from a pathname starts the path from the current directory.

Example: C>**CD LETTERS**

☑ List Filenames (DIR)

Use this procedure to view filenames and directory names, file sizes, and modification dates.

1. ■ To view all filenames in directory, type **DIR**, or
   ■ To view filenames that match wildcard criteria, type **DIR filename(s)**, or
   ■ To view all filenames on another drive, type **DIR drive:**, or
   ■ To view filenames by page, type **DIR /P**, or
   ■ To view filenames in wide screen format, type **DIR /W**
2. Press **ENTER**

Examples:
   A>**DIR**
   C>**DIR *.DOC**
   C>**DIR A:**
   C>**DIR A: /P**
   C>**DIR A: /W**

☑ Copy a File from One Floppy Disk to Another

1. Insert a formatted disk in target drive
2. Type **COPY drive:filename targetdrive:**
3. Press **ENTER**

Example:
   A>**COPY A:MEMO B:** (Copies MEMO from A: to B:.)

☑ Copy a File from a Floppy Disk to a Hard Disk

1. Change drive (e.g., **C:**) and directory (**CD**) to the hard disk drive and directory to contain the copied file
2. Type **COPY A:filename C:** (if the file is in A:)
3. Press **ENTER**

Example:
    C>**COPY A:JUNE.TXT C:** (Copies JUNE.TXT from A: to C:.)

☑ Copy a File from a Hard Disk to a Floppy Disk

1. Change drive (e.g., **C:**) and directory (**CD**) to the hard disk drive and directory containing the file to copy
2. Type **COPY filename A:** (if you are copying to A:)
3. Press **ENTER**

Example:
    C>**COPY BUDGET.DOC A:** (Copies BUDGET.DOC from C: to A:.)

☑ Copy a File Within the Same Disk

1. Change drive (e.g., **C:**) and directory (**CD**) to the drive and directory containing the file to copy
2. Type **COPY filename targetpath**
3. Press **ENTER**

Example:
A>**COPY MEMO C:\WORD** (Copies MEMO to WORD directory.)

☑ Copy All Files from One Floppy Disk to Another (COPY *.*)

1. Insert a formatted disk in target drive
2. Type **COPY sourcedisk:*.* targetdrive:**
3. Press **ENTER**

Examples:
A>**COPY A:*.* B:** (Copies all files in A: to B:)
A>**XCOPY A:\ B: /S** (Copies directories and files, creates directories if necessary.)

☑ Delete/Undelete a File

This procedure permanently deletes the indicated file from the disk or directory you specify.

1. Change drive (e.g., **C:**) and directory (**CD**) to the drive and directory containing the file to erase
2. Type **ERASE** (or **DEL**) **filename**
3. Press **ENTER**

Examples:
A>**ERASE MEMO3.DOC**
A>**DEL MEMO3.DOC**
A>**UNDELETE MEMO3.DOC** (DOS 5–6)

☑ Rename a File

1. Change drive (e.g., **C:**) and directory (**CD**) to the drive and directory containing the file to rename
2. Type **RENAME** (or **REN**) **oldname newname**
3. Press **ENTER**

Example: C>**REN DATA.92 DATA.93**

☑ Copy Entire Floppy Disk (DISKCOPY)

NOTE: This procedure erases all files on the target disk, formats the target disk if necessary, and copies an exact image of all files onto the target disk.

1. Insert DOS disk (may be a hard disk) and make that drive current (e.g., **A:**)
2. Type **DISKCOPY sourcedrive: targetdrive:**
3. Press **ENTER**
4. Insert disk(s) (you may now replace the DOS disk) and press any key to begin
5. If using a single floppy drive system, follow prompts to replace disks
6. When copy is completed, to copy another disk, type **Y**; or, type **N**

Examples:
Dual floppy drive system: A>**DISKCOPY A: B:**
Single floppy drive system: A>**DISKCOPY A: A:**

☑ Format a Floppy Disk

Use this procedure to prepare a floppy disk to contain files created in DOS. You can format a previously unused disk or a disk that has already been used. This procedure erases all files on a disk, reformats the disk, and checks for damaged sectors.

NOTE: Avoid Inadvertently formatting hard disks in Drive C: or D:! Make sure your target is correct.

1. Insert DOS disk (may be a hard disk) and make that drive current (e.g., **A:**)
2. Type **FORMAT targetdrive:**
3. Press **ENTER**

Examples:
    C>**FORMAT A:** (Formats disk in Drive A:.)
    A>**FORMAT B:** (Formats disk in Drive B:.)
    C>**UNFORMAT A:** (DOS 5–6)

☑ Make a Directory (MD)

1. Change to the directory to contain the new directory
2. To make new directory, type **MD newname** and press `ENTER`. See page 11 for naming rules.

Example:
```
C>CD \WORD
C>MD CLIENT2
```

☑ Rename a Directory (MOVE)

You cannot move a directory to a new location (i.e., the directory path of the newname must be the same as that of the oldname).

1. Type **MOVE oldname newname** and press `ENTER`

Examples:
```
MOVE CLIENT2 CLIENT4
MOVE C:\WORD\CLIENT2 C:\WORD\CLIENT4
```

☑ Remove a Directory (RD)

You cannot remove a directory while it contains files. If desired, save files first by copying them to another directory.

1. Change to the directory while it contains files. If desired, save files first by copying them to another directory.
2. To delete all files in the directory to remove, type **DEL directory** and press `ENTER`
3. To remove the directory, type **RD directory** and press `ENTER`

Example:
```
C>CD \WORD
C>DEL CLIENT4
C>RD CLIENT4
```

GLOSSARY

APPLICATION PROGRAM. Any program such as a word processor, spreadsheet, or database manager that contains its own set of commands and performs useful business, scientific, or home-use functions.

ASCII FILE. (Acronym for American Standard Code for Information Interchange) A file that is stored in line-by-line format and does not contain special characters beyond the first 128 ASCII characters. Acceptable characters include backspace, line feed, form feed, carriage return (represented as control characters) and shifted and unshifted typewriter keys. A **CTRL** **Z** (^Z) signals the end of an ASCII file.

AUTOEXEC.BAT. Batch file (stored in root of boot disk) that runs automatically when you boot your computer.

BACKUP. A copy of a file or disk. You should back up all your important files (with use of the COPY, DISKCOPY, or MSBACKUP commands) in case the original files become damaged.

BATCH FILE. ASCII file with .BAT extension that contains DOS commands and specialized programming commands. Create and run batch files to automate repeating commands or to instruct the user. See **AUTOEXEC.BAT**.

BIOS. Basic input/output system. Software routines contained mostly in ROM that communicate with and control your computer's components.

BIT. One of the eight "on-off" switches in a byte.

BOOT. (Bootstrap) When you start up your computer, a boot disk must be present in Drive A: or the hard disk must be bootable. The boot disk contains DOS programs that enable your computer to start.

BUFFER. An area of your computer's memory that DOS sets aside for copying in parts of long files or programs. DOS then reads the information directly from memory, thus saving the time it would take to read the disk.

BYTE. One character of information such as a letter, space, or other ASCII character. The amount of information on a disk or in your computer's memory is measured in bytes, kilobytes (1,024 bytes), or megabytes (1,048,576 bytes).

COMMAND PROCESSOR. The program that communicates with you and sends your commands to DOS. COMMAND.COM contains internal DOS commands, displays error messages, and runs programs for you.

CONCATENATE. Append one or more files together into one file.

CONFIGURE. To set up DOS to operate effectively with your computer or to set up your computer to operate effectively with DOS.

CURRENT. DOS can have only one directory open per drive. When you change to a directory, you open it, or make it current. You can then access program and data files on that drive without specifying a full pathname from root.

DEVICE. A component to your computer that can be used for the input or output of information, e.g., disk drive, monitor, keyboard, mouse, printer.

DEVICE DRIVER. A .SYS file that tells DOS how to interact with a particular device. Specify necessary driver names in CONFIG.SYS.

DIRECTORY. A named subdivision of a disk used in organizing files. Each directory can contain subdirectories.

DISK CACHING. Software that stores information in memory that needs to be read from or sent to a disk and accesses the disk when the drive is not active. This allows programs quicker access to the disk.

DISK DRIVE. A mechanical device for holding, reading from, and writing to either a floppy or hard disk of magnetically stored information.

DOS DISK. A floppy disk or hard disk with Disk Operating System files including hidden operating system files, the COMMAND.COM file, any desired external DOS command files, and an optional AUTOEXEC.BAT file. The DOS disk may also contain other program or data files, if desired. You can boot your computer with a DOS disk.

ENVIRONMENT. A small area of RAM set aside by DOS to contain string information which can be read by DOS or other programs. Information includes PATH, PROMPT, location of COMMAND.COM, etc. View and modify the environment with the SET command.

EXPANDED MEMORY (EMS). Additional computer memory created by an add-on board to your computer or by configuring EXTENDED MEMORY. EMS requires an area (page frame) of the Upper Memory Area (between 640K and 1024K) to point to areas (pages) of expanded memory. EMS also requires a program called an expanded memory manager to operate. Only programs specifically designed to use expanded memory can access it.

EXTENDED MEMORY (XMS). Any memory capacity on your computer above the conventional memory range of 640 kilobytes. DOS can load programs into XMS to free up conventional memory. The HIMEM.SYS program is an extended memory manager that prevents programs from addressing the same registers in extended memory. Memory between 640K and 1024K is called Upper Memory Area (UMA) and is used mostly by your hardware, although you can load some programs into UMA. High Memory Area (HMA) is memory above 1024K into which you can also load programs.

EXTERNAL COMMANDS. Infrequently used DOS commands that are not stored in memory. To issue an external command, either the directory containing the external command file must be current, or you must specify a pathname before the command verb, or the command file must be located in the system PATH.

FILE. A unit of stored information identified by a filename. A file can be either a data file (e.g., text document, spreadsheet, picture) or an executing file (e.g., word processor, spreadsheet program, game).

FILENAME. The eight-character name that identifies a file. A filename can contain an optional three-character extension preceded by a period. Example: **AUTOEXEC.BAT MYLIST.12**

FILE SPECIFICATION. When issuing certain DOS commands, you can indicate a file specification parameter by typing either a filename or a filename including wildcards (* or ?).

FILTER. A program which requires input from a file or program, changes the information in some way, and produces output.

FIXED DISK. See **HARD DISK**.

FLOPPY DISK. (Also called "diskette") A flat, removable disk inside a flexible cover. The disk stores information and programs magnetically and retains the information even after your computer is turned off.

FORMAT. For DOS to be able to read or write to a disk, the disk must have been previously "formatted" by DOS; that is, contain system tracks created with the FORMAT command. Note: the FORMAT command erases all files currently stored on a disk.

HARD DISK. (Also called "fixed disk" or "rigid disk") A three-dimensional usually non-removable cylinder containing magnetic media that stores information and programs even after your computer is turned off.

HARDWARE. Your computer and its various components such as monitor, keyboard, disk drives, memory, and modem. Computer hardware allows you to run software programs, view the results, and create new data or programs.

HIGH-CAPACITY DISK. A floppy disk that contains information that can only be read by a high-capacity disk drive.

INTERNAL COMMANDS. Frequently used DOS commands that are placed in memory when you boot your computer. You can issue internal commands no matter which directory is current.

LOGGED DRIVE. The disk drive you are currently using, as indicated by the DOS prompt (e.g., A>).

MEMORY. A component of your computer that holds data, programs, DOS buffers, and DOS environment information for as long as your computer is powered up. Data in memory is manipulated by programs. The amount of available memory space determines the size of programs and data files you can use and the number of programs you can have resident.

OPERATING SYSTEM. The software necessary to boot your computer, manage your files, and configure your computer.

PARALLEL PORT. A multi-wire connector (PRN, LPT1:, or LPT2:) on your computer that allows DOS to communicate with devices such as printers one full byte at a time. See also **SERIAL PORT**.

PARAMETER. A file specification or text string that you type on the DOS command line to supply necessary information for the specified command or program.

PARENT DIRECTORY. A directory that contains a subdirectory is the parent to that subdirectory.

PATH. Command that tells DOS in which drives or directories to find programs or external commands.

PATHNAME. Part of a drive specifier or filename that specifies the exact drive and directory of a file. Separate directory names with a \.

PIPING. The operation of sending the output of one program into the input of another.

QUEUE. A line of print jobs initiated by the PRINT command and waiting in turn to be printed.

RAM. (Acronym for Random Access Memory) Main part of your computer's memory where DOS temporarily copies data and program files for processing. These files are erased when you turn off your computer.

REDIRECTION. The operation of temporarily changing the standard input or standard output of a command or program.

ROM. (Acronym for Read-Only Memory) A small part of your computer's memory that usually contains machine use programs and that cannot be erased, even when you turn off your computer.

ROOT DIRECTORY. The main directory that contains all of a disk's subdirectories.

SERIAL PORT. A connector (COM1: or COM2:) on your computer (using as few as two wires) through which DOS communicates with devices such as a serial printer, modem, or mouse one bit at a time. See also **PARALLEL PORT**.

SOFTWARE. Programs stored as magnetic files. Operating system software such as PC-DOS activates your computer hardware and enables you to manage files. See **APPLICATION PROGRAM**.

STANDARD INPUT. The assumed source of information (usually the keyboard). Use redirection to change the standard input.

STANDARD OUTPUT: The assumed destination of information (usually the monitor). Use redirection to change the standard output.

VOLUME. A name for a disk. Each disk can be considered a volume with an optional identifying label which you can view with VOL, LABEL, or DIR.

WILDCARD. A special character in a file specification that stands for any character(s) in its place. This enables you to refer to several files at once or to refer to a file whose full name you do not remember. DOS wildcards include * and ?.

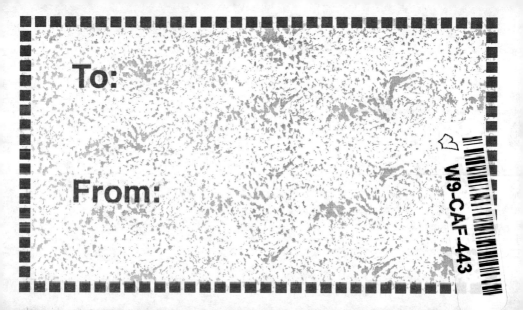

To:

From:

W9-CAF-443

CASSEROLES
fast and easy

Printed in the United States of America

ISBN 1-56383-009-4

TABLE OF CONTENTS

GROUND BEEF

BARLEY HOT DISH

1½ lbs. ground beef
1 C. chopped onion
½ C. chopped celery
3 T. oil
½ bay leaf
1-10½ oz. can cream of
 mushroom soup
¾ C. barley

1-1 lb. can peas
2½ tsp. salt
¼ tsp. pepper
1 tsp. marjoram
2-1 lb. cans tomatoes
2½ C. water
½ C. chopped green pepper

Preheat oven to 375°. Saute ground beef, onion and celery in hot oil in Dutch oven until browned. Stir in remaining ingredients; mix well. Bring mixture to a boil. Turn into buttered shallow 15x10⅝x2" roasting pan (4-quart). Cover with foil or lid. Bake at 375° for 1¼ hours or until barley is tender. Add extra water if necessary. Makes 10 servings.

SPANISH RICE

1 C. raw rice
1 medium onion, chopped
½ medium green pepper,
  chopped
½ lb. ground beef
2-8 oz. cans tomato sauce

1¾ C. hot water
1 tsp. dry mustard
½ tsp. salt
¼ tsp. pepper
¼ C. Wesson oil

Heat Wesson oil in pan, add rice and brown slightly. Add onion, pepper and ground beef. Stir until meat is slightly browned. Add tomato sauce, water and seasonings. Bring to boil and then simmer on low heat 25 minutes. Makes 4 servings.

BEEF AND EGGPLANT CASSEROLE

2 tsp. butter
3 T. butter
¼ C. minced onion
2 medium eggplants, pared
  cut into 1" cubes (about
  6 C.)
1½ tsp. salt
Dash of dried thyme

1 C. evaporated milk
½ C. fresh bread crumbs
1 clove garlic, grated
1 lb. ground beef
Dash of pepper
1 can condensed tomato
  soup

Preheat oven to 375°. Melt 2 teaspoons butter In skillet; toss with crumbs; set aside on waxed paper. In same skillet, in 3 tablespoons butter, lightly brown garlic, onions and ground beef. Add eggplant, salt, pepper and thyme; cook over low heat 10 minutes. Stir in soup and milk. Pour mixture into 2-quart buttered casserole. Cover with crumbs. Bake 25 to 30 minutes or until crumbs are browned.

3

HAMBURGER-HARVEST CASSEROLE

1 lb. ground chuck
1 C. minced onion
1-#2 can tomatoes
1 T. Worcestershire sauce
2 tsp. salt
2 C. thinly sliced raw
  potatoes
⅓ C. flour

1 pkg. frozen corn, thawed
  enough to separate
1 pkg. frozen limas, thawed
  to separate
1 green pepper, slivered
1½ C. Cheddar cheese,
  grated, (6 oz.)

Preheat oven to 375°. Combine beef, onions, tomatoes, Worcestershire and salt. Pat into 1" layer in 3-quart buttered casserole. On top, place in layers, potatoes, flour, corn, limas, then green pepper. Bake, covered, 45 minutes; then sprinkle with cheese; bake uncovered 30 minutes longer, or until vegetables are tender. Makes 8 servings.

COMPANY CASSEROLE

½ lb. medium-wide noodles
1 T. butter
1 lb. ground chuck
2-8 oz. cans tomato sauce
1-8 oz. pkg. cream cheese
1 C. cottage cheese

¼ C. sour cream
⅓ C. minced onion
1 T. minced green pepper
2 T. melted butter or
  margarine
Salt and pepper to taste

Preheat oven to 375°. Cook noodles according to package directions; drain. Saute beef until brown; season; stir in tomato sauce. Combine cheeses, sour cream, onion and pepper. Spread half of noodles in 2-quart buttered casserole; cover with cheese mixture; cover with rest of noodles. Drizzle melted butter over; cover with tomato-meat mixture. Bake 45 minutes. Serves 6 generously.

5

CROWN CASSEROLE

1 lb. ground beef
1 pkg. frozen, mixed
   vegetables
1/3 C. chopped green pepper
1-3/4 oz. pkg. brown gravy
   mix

1 1/4 C. hot water
Dash of garlic powder
1/3 C. mayonnaise
1-8 oz. can refrigerated
   biscuits
Dash of salt

Preheat oven to 425°. Brown beef, add salt, vegetables, green pepper, gravy mix, hot water, garlic powder and bring to boil. Remove from heat; stir in mayonnaise. Place mixture in 1 1/2-quart buttered casserole. Flatten biscuits slightly and lay on top of mixture. Brush biscuits with additional mayonnaise. Bake until biscuits are browned, 15 minutes.

HAMBURGER CABBAGE CASSEROLE

2 lbs. ground beef
1 large onion, chopped
6 T. rice, raw
¾ C. cubed cheese

2-10½ oz. cans tomato soup
2 cans (soup) water
4 to 6 C. shredded cabbage
1 sliced carrot

Preheat oven to 350°. Brown ground beef and onion together; add soup and water; stir. Add rice and simmer 5 minutes. Arrange cabbage in bottom of 9x13" buttered pan. Add carrot and cubed cheese on top. Pour meat mixture over all this. <u>Do not stir</u>; cover and bake 1½ hours.

CHEF'S CASSEROLE

8 oz. wide noodles
1½ lbs. ground beef
1 large onion, chopped
1 tsp. salt
Dash of pepper

1-15 oz. can tomato sauce
3 oz. can mushrooms,
 undrained
8 oz. pkg. sliced, sharp
 American cheese

Preheat oven to 350°. Cook noodles as directed on package; drain well. Lightly brown ground beef and onion. Add salt and pepper, tomato sauce, chopped mushrooms with liquid, and 4 slices cubed cheese. Turn into 13x9x2" greased baking dish. Bake, uncovered, in oven 30 to 35 minutes. Arrange remaining 4 slices of cheese over top of casserole. Return to oven until cheese is melted. Makes 8 to 10 servings.

HEARTY CASSEROLE

1 lb. ground beef
½ C. chopped onion
½ C. chopped celery
1 C. rice, cooked
  (this will equal 3 C. rice)

1-10½ oz. can cream of
  chicken soup
1-10½ oz. can cream of
  mushroom soup
1 can water
1 T. Worcestershire sauce
1 small can chow mein
  noodles

Preheat oven to 350°. Place ground beef, onion and celery in skillet; cook until browned. Add rice, soups, water and Worcestershire sauce; stir together and put in greased 2-quart casserole. Top with chow mein noodles and bake 40 to 45 minutes.

EASY CASSEROLE

1 lb. ground beef
1-10½ oz. can cream of
   mushroom or cream of
   celery soup

1 box mixed frozen
   vegetables
Tater tots

Preheat oven to 350°. Press ground beef into 8" buttered baking pan. Pour over this the can of undiluted soup. Spread frozen vegetables over soup and cover with tater tots. Bake 45 to 50 minutes.

SKILLET DINNER

1 lb. ground beef
¼ C. chopped onion
1 C. cooked macaroni
2-8 oz. cans tomato sauce

1-12 oz. can whole kernel
corn
2 tsp. chili powder
½ tsp. seasoned salt
½ C. diced Cheddar cheese

Brown beef and onions in large skillet. Pour off any fat and stir in cooked macaroni, tomato sauce, corn, chili powder and seasoned salt. Simmer, stirring occasionally for 5 to 10 minutes. Stir in cheese and serve immediately. Stove top - medium heat. Makes 4 servings.

HANDY HOT DISH

2 T. onion, chopped
2 T. celery, chopped
1 tsp. salt
⅛ tsp. pepper
2 T. chopped red pepper
1 C. seasoned buttered
   bread crumbs

2 T. butter
1 lb. ground beef
1 C. rice, raw
2 cans cream of chicken
   soup
2 cans hot water

Preheat oven to 325°. Cook onion and celery in butter until tender. Add ground beef and cook until redness disappears. Turn into buttered 2-quart casserole dish. Stir in rice, salt and pepper. Combine soup and hot water and heat to boiling in skillet and pour over rice mixture. Fold in red pepper. Bake at 325°, 2 hours, stirring several times. Toward the end of the baking, sprinkle with buttered crumbs. Continue baking until crumbs are delicately browned.

12

HOMESPUN MEAT PIE

1 lb. ground beef
4 oz. can mushrooms, drained
1 egg
⅓ C. chopped onion
¼ C. dry bread crumbs
Salt and pepper to taste

2 C. chopped potatoes, cooked
3 T. milk
½ lb. cheese, grated (American or sharp Cheddar)
1 T. parsley
¼ tsp. salt

Preheat oven to 400°. Combine meat, mushrooms, egg, onion, bread crumbs and seasonings. Mix lightly. Press meat mixture onto bottom and sides of a 9" pie plate. Bake at 400°, 15 minutes. Mash hot potatoes with milk, stir in cheese, parsley and salt. Remove meat shell from oven. Reduce oven temperature to 350°. Fill shell with potato mixture. Bake for 10 more minutes. Makes 6 servings.

13

A MAN'S CASSEROLE

4 C. medium noodles (¼ lb.)
3 or 4 medium onions,
  chopped
2 T. butter
2 lbs. ground chuck
1 T. oil
2 tsp. salt

½ tsp. pepper
1 tsp. thyme
1 can cream of celery soup,
  undiluted
½ C. milk
1½ C. grated Cheddar or
  sharp cheese
3 eggs, beaten

Preheat oven to 350°. Cook noodles according to directions; drain. In large skillet, saute onions in butter until tender; set aside. In same skillet, cook beef in oil with salt, pepper, thyme, stirring to break meat into bits, about 10 minutes or until meat loses color; add sauteed onion. In 3-quart buttered casserole, arrange 1/3 of noodles, then half of meat mixture and half of soup combined with milk. Repeat and put last of noodles on top. Sprinkle cheese over this and pour beaten eggs on top of cheese. Bake, covered, until hot and bubbly (top will be very crisp), 1 hour. Makes 8 to 10 servings.

PLENTY MORE IN KITCHEN CASSEROLE

2 lbs. ground beef
1 C. chopped onion
2-4 oz. cans tomato sauce
2-4 oz. cans mushrooms
1 can mushroom soup
1-12 oz. can whole kernel
  corn

1 T. Worcestershire sauce
2 tsp. salt
1 T. chili powder
1 T. brown sugar
1 C. shredded Cheddar
  cheese
1-8 oz. pkg. macaroni,
  cooked

Preheat oven to 350°. Brown ground beef and onion; add the rest of ingredients, but omit the cooked macaroni. Simmer for 10 minutes, then add the cooked macaroni and bake 1 hour in greased 9x13" pan. Makes 8 to 10 servings.

HAMBURGER CASSEROLE

2 lbs. ground beef
3 eggs, beaten
2 tsp. salt
¼ tsp. pepper
2 T. onion, chopped

½ C. catsup
2 C. milk
1 C. Cheddar cheese
2⅔ C. Potato Buds

Preheat oven to 350°. Mix all ingredients together except the Potato Buds and cheese. Put into 9x13" pan and bake 1 hour. Mix 2⅔ cups Potato Buds according to directions on package (8-serving size). Spread on baked meat, sprinkle with cheese. Bake 10 to 15 minutes or until cheese melts.

WILD RICE AND HAMBURGER CASSEROLE

⅓ pkg. wild rice
1 can mushroom soup
1 can cream of chicken
  soup
⅓ C. milk
1 can sliced mushrooms,
  drained

1 lb. ground beef
1 onion, chopped
1 tsp. Worcestershire sauce
2 T. green pepper, chopped
¼ C. slivered almonds

Soak wild rice overnight in water. Drain and cook 20 minutes in boiling water. Drain. Add soups, milk and mushrooms. Brown beef and onions in heavy skillet, add remaining ingredients. Combine rice and meat mixture. Place in buttered 9x13" pan and bake 30 minutes in preheated 375° oven. Makes 8 to 10 servings.

HAMBURGER-CORN CASSEROLE

1½ lbs. ground beef
1 C. chopped onion
1-12 oz. can whole kernel
  corn, drained
1 can cream of chicken
  soup
1 can cream of mushroom
  soup

1 C. dairy sour cream
¼ C. chopped pimento
¾ tsp. salt
¼ tsp. pepper
3 C. medium cooked
  noodles
1 C. soft bread crumbs
3 T. butter, melted

Preheat oven to 350°. Brown beef. Add onion; cook until tender, but not brown. Add next 7 ingredients, mix well. Stir in noodles. Pour into 2-quart buttered casserole. Mix crumbs and butter; sprinkle over top. Bake 30 minutes. Makes 8 to 10 servings.

HAMBURGER SKILLET STEW

1 lb. ground beef
¼ C. fine dry bread crumbs
¼ C. chopped onion
1 egg
1½ tsp. salt
¼ tsp. pepper
1 T. Worcestershire sauce
1 T. flour

2-8 oz. cans tomato sauce
2 T. vegetalbe oil
1 large onion quartered
4 medium carrots, sliced
2 small potatoes, quartered
1 C. water
1 tsp. salt
1 pkg. frozen green beans

Combine beef, bread crumbs, onion, egg, 1½ teaspoons salt, pepper, Worcestershire sauce and ½ cup tomato sauce. Shape into 16 balls. Brown in hot oil in large skillet. Add quartered onion, carrots and potatoes, water and 1 teaspoon salt. Pour in remaining tomato sauce. Cover, simmer 1 hour, stirring occasionally. Add beans in last 30 minutes cooking time. Remove ½ cup stew sauce; blend in flour. Gradually pour into stew, stirring over low heat until it thickens.

CHILI CASSEROLE

3 lbs. ground beef
3 C. chopped onion
3 pkgs. chili seasoning mix
3-8 oz. cans tomato sauce
2 C. water
3-1 lb. cans kidney beans,
 drained

1-3¾ oz. pkg. small corn
 chips
¾ C. sliced, pitted black
 olives
1½ C. shredded sharp
 Cheddar cheese

Preheat oven to 325°. In large skillet, cook meat until it loses its red color, breaking up with fork. Add onion, seasoning mix, tomato sauce and water. Stir, bring to boil, cover and simmer for 15 minutes, stirring several times to prevent sticking. Add beans, corn chips and cheese. Put into 4-quart buttered casserole and bake 50 to 60 minutes. Makes 12 servings.

JIFFY CHILI-HOMINY BAKE

1 lb. ground beef
½ C. chopped onion
1-15 oz. can chili with beans
1 T. chili powder
1-10½ oz. can cream of
  chicken soup

1-1 lb. 4 oz. can yellow
  hominy, drained
2 T. ripe olives, sliced
2 oz. American cheese,
  shredded

Preheat oven to 350°. Cook beef and onion until beef loses redness. Stir in remaining ingredients, except cheese. Turn into greased 2-quart casserole. Cover, bake 25 minutes. Sprinkle cheese on top. Bake, uncovered, 5 minutes longer. Makes 6 servings.

BEANIE MAC CASSEROLE

1 T. butter
1 C. chopped onion
1 tsp. salt
1 lb. ground beef
¾ tsp. chili powder
¼ tsp. pepper

1-16 oz. can kidney beans
1-1 lb. 12 oz. can tomatoes
1-10½ oz. can bisque of
  tomato soup
6 oz. macaroni, uncooked

Preheat oven to 350°. Cook butter, chopped onion, salt, ground beef, chili powder and pepper until ground beef loses redness. Add rest of ingredients and put into 2-quart casserole and bake 1 hour and 15 minutes. Casserole should be covered while baking.

CALICO BEAN CASSEROLE

½ lb. ground beef
½ lb. bacon, cut into small
  pieces
1-15 oz. can butter beans
1-15 oz. can pork and beans
1-15 oz. can kidney beans
½ C. chopped onion

½ C. white sugar
½ C. brown sugar
1 T. vinegar
1 tsp. mustard (dry)
½ C. catsup
¼ tsp. salt
¼ tsp. pepper

Preheat oven to 350°. Fry ground beef and bacon together. Mix all the ingredients together. Place in a 2-quart buttered casserole and bake for 45 minutes.

CHEESE MACARONI MEDLEY

1 C. macaroni
½ tsp. salt
1 C. chopped onion
1-4 oz. can mushrooms,
  drained
2 T. flour
2 C. milk
1-14½ oz. can sliced baby
  tomatoes, drained

1 lb. ground beef
¼ tsp. pepper
1 C. green pepper strips
2 T. butter
½ tsp. salt
1-10 oz. pkg. shredded
  Cheddar cheese (2½ C.)
½ C. shredded Cheddar
  cheese

Preheat oven to 350°. Cook macaroni boiling, salted water 15 minutes. Drain well. Meanwhile, cook ground beef, ½ teaspoon salt and pepper in 12" skillet until meat turns color. Add onion, green pepper and mushrooms. Bring to boil; set aside. Melt butter in 2-quart saucepan. Stir in flour and ½ teaspoon salt. Cook 1 minute, stirring constantly. Gradually stir in milk. Cook until thickened. Remove from heat. Stir in 2½ cups cheese. Combine sauce with meat mixture. Add macaroni; mix gently. Put into greased 11x7x1½" baking dish. Top with tomatoes and ½ cup cheese. Bake 30 minutes. Makes 8 servings.

GROUND BEEF STROGANOFF

2 T. butter
1 lb. ground beef
½ C. chopped onion
1 clove garlic, minced
  or 1 T. garlic salt
1 T. flour

1-10½ oz. can cream of
  chicken soup
1-4 oz. can mushrooms,
  undrained
1 tsp. salt
¼ tsp. pepper
1 C. dairy sour cream
1 large can chow mein
  noodles

In large skillet, melt butter; add ground beef, onion and garlic. Cook until meat is done. Stir in flour, then add soup, mushrooms, salt and pepper. Stir in sour cream and heat to serving temperature. Serve over noodles or stir noodles into mixture.

BEEF STROGANOFF

2 lbs. ground beef
¾ C. chopped onion
1½ tsp. garlic salt
¼ tsp. pepper
½ C. flour

1-4 oz. can mushrooms,
  undrained
2-10½ oz. cans cream of
  mushroom soup
3 C. chow mein noodles
1 small carton sour cream

Combine ground beef, onion, garlic salt and pepper in 3-quart Dutch oven. Cook until beef loses redness. Add flour and stir in well. Add undrained mushrooms and soup. Stir well and bring to a bubbling heat. Add sour cream and chow mein noodles. Stir well and serve. Makes 8 servings.

STROGANOFF CASSEROLE

1 lb. ground beef
1-10½ oz. can cream of
  mushroom soup
¼ tsp. pepper
1 C. dairy sour cream

⅓ C. oil
1 C. chopped onion
1 tsp. salt
1-17 oz. can sweet peas
1-7 oz. pkg. macaroni

Preheat oven to 350°. Cook macaroni according to directions. Drain. Combine ground beef, onion and seasonings and shape into 16 meatballs. Brown the meatballs in oil, turning to brown all sides. Stir in soup; cover and simmer 10 minutes. Remove from heat; stir in sour cream, macaroni and sweet peas. Put in greased 2-quart casserole dish and bake 45 minutes. Makes 8 servings.

ALL-AT-ONCE SPAGHETTI DINNER

1 lb. ground beef
1 medium onion, chopped
3-8 oz. cans tomato sauce
1½ C. water
¼ tsp. pepper

¼ tsp. ground oregano
1½ C. sliced ripe olives
½ lb. spaghetti, uncooked
1 C. Cheddar cheese,
 shredded

Cook and stir beef and onion in a heavy 3-quart saucepan until meat loses red color. Stir In seasonings and olives. Pour in 3 cans tomato sauce and water. Bring to boil. Break uncooked spaghetti in half, sprinkle in a little at a time, stirring into the sauce. Cover tightly and simmer 25 to 30 minutes over low heat. Stir in Cheddar cheese until cheese is melted.

LASAGNA CASSEROLE

2 tsp. seasoned salt
1 lb. ground beef
2 cloves garlic, crushed
½ tsp. pepper
1-#2½ can tomatoes
  (3½ C.)
1-8 oz. can tomato sauce

1 pkg. spaghetti sauce mix
½ lb. lasagna noodles
½ lb. mozzarella cheese,
  sliced
½ lb. ricotta cheese
  (carefully drained cottage
  cheese may replace
  ricotta)
½ C. grated Parmesan
  cheese

Preheat oven to 350°. In seasoned salt, in hot Dutch oven or deep kettle, brown beef. Add crushed garlic and pepper; simmer slowly, uncovered, 10 minutes. Stir in tomatoes, tomato sauce and spaghetti sauce mix; cover and simmer 30 minutes. Meanwhile, cook lasagna noodles in salted, boiling water until tender; drain. In 12x8x2" buttered pan, pour ⅓ of sauce; cover with strips of lasagna noodles; then over lasagna noodles arrange slices of mozzarella and spoonfuls of ricotta. Repeat layers, ending with meat sauce, then top with Parmesan cheese. Bake 20 minutes. Makes 6 to 8 servings.

TOSTADA-STYLE LASAGNE

2 lbs. ground beef
1-28 oz. can tomatoes, cut
1 tsp. oregano
½ tsp. red pepper
1½ tsp. salt
½ C. chopped onion
1-8 oz. can tomato sauce
1 tsp. chili powder

1-15½ oz. can red kidney
  beans, drained
8 lasagne noodles, cooked,
  drained and halved
  crosswise
4 C. shredded Monterey
  Jack cheese
Shredded lettuce
Broken tortilla chips
Cherry tomatoes, halved

Preheat oven to 350°. Cook meat and onion until meat is brown and onion tender. Stir in undrained tomatoes, tomato sauce, 1½ teaspoons salt, oregano, chili powder and red pepper. Simmer, uncovered, 25 minutes. Stir occasionally. Stir in beans, In 2-10x6x2" greased casserole, arrange ¼ of cooked noodles and spread with ¼ of meat mixture. Sprinkle ½ of cheese atop each. Top with remaining noodles and meat mixture. Bake, covered, 15 minutes. Uncover and bake 10 more minutes. To serve, pass lettuce, chips and tomatoes to sprinkle atop. Makes 4 to 6 servings each.

CHEESE LOAVES

2 lbs. ground beef
2¾ C. fresh bread crumbs
½ C. onion, chopped
½ C. green pepper, chopped
1 tsp. salt

¼ tsp. pepper
1 can vegetable soup
¼ C. milk
½ lb. Swiss cheese, cut into
  16 cubes
1 lb. can meatless Ragu
  spaghetti sauce

Preheat oven to 400°. Mix first 8 ingredients well. Form balls or rolls around cubed Swiss cheese and put in 9x13" pan. Cover with spaghetti sauce and bake 1 hour. Makes 8 to 10 servings.

POTATO PIZZA SUPREME

1 lb. ground beef
½ C. onion, chopped
¼ tsp. pepper
15 oz. can tomato sauce
4 C. thinly sliced potatoes
1 can Cheddar cheese soup
½ C. Parmesan cheese

8 oz. pkg. mozzarella
  cheese
½ tsp. salt
½ tsp. oregano
½ tsp. sugar
½ C. milk
1 T. butter

Preheat oven to 375°. Brown beef in pan. Add all ingredients but tomato sauce and cheese. Put in 9x13" greased pan. Pour tomato sauce over and bake at 375°, 45 to 60 minutes. Add cheeses on top and return to oven 15 minutes. Makes 8 to 10 servings.

POTATO PIZZA BAKE

1 lb. ground beef
4 C. thinly sliced potatoes
1 medium onion, sliced thin
1 can Cheddar cheese soup
1 can milk, soup can
1-15 oz. can tomato sauce

Salt and pepper to taste
½ tsp. oregano
½ tsp. sugar
1 T. butter
6 oz. sliced mozzarella
  cheese
½ C. Parmesan cheese

Preheat oven to 375°. Cook ground beef in skillet until it loses redness. Place potatoes and onions in buttered 9x13" pan. Add meat to mixture. Mix cheese soup and milk until smooth and add to meat and potatoes; mix together. Combine tomato sauce, salt, pepper, oregano and sugar. Pour sauce over the top, but do not mix. Dot with butter. Cover pan with foil. Bake at 375° for 1 hour. Remove cover and arrange sliced cheese on top. Sprinkle with Parmesan. Return to oven, uncovered, for about 15 minutes or until cheese bubbles.

TATER TOT CASSEROLE

2 lbs. ground beef
1 large onion, chopped
½ C. celery
1-10½ oz. can cream of
chicken or celery soup

1-10½ oz. can cream of
mushroom soup
Tater tots

Preheat oven to 350°. Brown ground beef and onion. Add celery and soups.
Place in 2-quart buttered casserole and cover with as many tater tots as you
can get on. This is quick, easy and kids love it. Bake 30 minutes.

ITALIAN DELIGHT

1 lb. ground beef	1 can tomato soup
1 onion, chopped fine	1 can corn niblets
1 green pepper, chopped fine	1 small can button mushrooms
1 clove garlic, chopped fine	½ lb. cooked spaghetti
¼ C. oil	1 C. grated Cheddar cheese

Preheat oven to 350°. Brown beef in oil; add onion, pepper and garlic; cook 10 minutes. Add remaining ingredients except cheese and place in 1½-quart buttered casserole. Sprinkle cheese on top and bake 1 hour. Makes 6 servings.

SPOON-BREAD TAMALE BAKE

¼ C. oil
1½ lbs. ground chuck
1 C. chopped onion
1 clove garlic, minced
½ C. chopped green pepper
1-#2 can tomatoes
1-12 oz. can whole kernel
  corn
1½ C. milk
2 T. butter

1 C. grated Cheddar cheese
1 T. salt
1½ T. chili powder
¼ tsp. pepper
½ C. corn meal
1 C. water
1 C. pitted ripe olives
1 tsp. salt
½ C. corn meal
2 eggs, lightly beaten

Preheat oven to 375°. Place oil in skillet, brown beef, add onions, garlic, green pepper; cook, stirring, until onions are golden. Stir in tomatoes, corn, 1 tablespoon salt, chili powder and pepper; simmer 5 minutes. Stir in ½ cup corn meal mixed with water; cover; simmer 10 minutes. Add olives, put into 3-quart buttered casserole. Meanwhile, heat milk with 1 teaspoon salt and butter; slowly stir in ½ cup corn meal; cook, stirring until thickened. Remove from heat, stir in cheese and eggs; pour over meat mixture in casserole. Bake 30 to 40 minutes. Makes 6 to 8 servings.

EASY ITALIAN CASSEROLE

1 lb. ground beef
1 clove garlic, crushed
1-4 oz. can mushrooms,
  drained
½ tsp. oregano leaves
¼ tsp. salt
2 C. Bisquick baking mix
1 egg

¼ C. Parmesan cheese
½ C. chopped onion
1-16 oz. can tomato sauce
1 tsp. sugar
½ tsp. basil leaves
¼ tsp. pepper
½ C. milk
8 slices American cheese

Preheat oven to 400°. Cook and stir beef, onion and garlic until brown; drain. Stir in sauce, mushrooms, sugar, oregano, basil, salt and pepper. Heat to boiling; reduce heat, simmer 10 minutes. Mix baking mix, milk and egg; spread half in an 8x8x2" greased pan. Top with 4 cheese slices. Spoon beef over cheese. Top with remaining cheese slices; sprinkle with Parmesan cheese. Drop remaining dough by spoonfuls onto cheese. Sprinkle with paprika. Bake for 20 minutes. Makes 6 to 8 servings.

SUMMER MEATBALL STEW

1 lb. ground chuck
¼ C. chopped parsley
¼ C. milk
½ tsp. oregano
½ C. soft bread crumbs
1 egg
¾ tsp. salt
¼ tsp. pepper
2 T. oil
1½ C. green pepper strips
1 clove garlic, minced

1-28 oz. can tomatoes
2 C. water
½ tsp. basil leaves
½ lb. fresh mushrooms,
 sliced
1 C. chopped onion
½ lb. fresh green beans, cut
 into 2" pieces
1 beef bouillon cube
1 tsp. oregano
1 lb. zucchini, sliced

Combine first 8 ingredients in bowl. Mix lightly, but well. Shape into 24 meatballs. Heat oil in skillet over medium heat. Brown meatballs on all sides. Remove meatballs from skillet. Add mushrooms, green pepper, onion and garlic. Saute 10 minutes or until tender. Pour off excess fat. Stir in meatballs, green beans, tomatoes, bouillon cube, water, 1 teaspoon oregano and basil. Cook until mixture comes to a boil, about 2 minutes. Reduce heat to low. Cover and simmer 15 minutes. Add zucchini. Cover, simmer 20 minutes or until tender. Stove top - 1 hour. Makes 8 servings.

MEATBALL AND BEAN STEW

1 lb. ground beef
½ C. fresh bread crumbs
¼ C. minced onion
3 T. fresh parsley
1 tsp. salt
½ tsp. oregano leaves
2-1 lb. 1 oz. cans kidney
  beans
1 lb. 12 oz. can Italian
  tomatoes, cut up
1-15 oz. can tomato sauce

1 bay leaf
½ tsp. oregano leaves
½ tsp. basil leaves
Shredded Cheddar cheese
¼ tsp. basil leaves
1 egg
¼ C. milk
2 T. oil
1 C. green pepper strips

Combine ground beef, bread crumbs, onion, parsley, salt, ½ teaspoon oregano, ¼ teaspoon basil, egg and milk in bowl. Mix lightly, but well. Shape into 32 meatballs. Brown in hot oil in Dutch oven; remove as they brown. Pour off all but 2 tablespoons fat. Saute green pepper in fat until tender. Add remaining ingredients except cheese; mix well. Add meatballs and simmer, uncovered, 30 minutes. Serve in bowls topped with cheese. Makes 10 servings.

BEEF AND MUSHROOM CASSEROLE

1½ lbs. ground beef
¼ C. chopped onion
1 tsp. marjoram leaves
1 egg
⅓ C. cooking oil
½ C. chopped onion
1½ C. cooked carrots, drained
½ C. milk
3 C. mashed instant potatoes

½ C. dry bread crumbs
2 tsp. salt
¼ tsp. pepper
½ C. milk
1-8 oz. can mushrooms
1-10 oz. can cream of mushroom soup
1 T. Worcestershire sauce
1-10 oz. pkg. frozen peas, cooked and drained
Paprika

50

Preheat oven to 350°. Combine ground beef, bread crumbs, ¼ cup onion, salt, marjoram, pepper, egg and ½ cup milk. Mix well. Shape mixture into 36 meatballs. Brown a few meatballs at a time on all sides in hot oil. Remove. Drain mushrooms, reserve liquid. Saute mushrooms and ½ cup onion in pan drippings until onions are tender. Stir in soup, ½ cup milk, Worcestershire sauce and reserved mushroom liquid. Bring to a boil. Arrange meatballs, carrots and peas in a 3-quart casserole. Pour sauce over all. Spoon mashed potatoes around edge of casserole and bake 30 minutes. Makes 8 servings.

MEATBALL CASSEROLE

½ lb. ground beef
½ C. cracker crumbs
1 egg
¼ C. chopped onion
¼ tsp. salt
2 T. oil
2 C. cooked rice

Dash of pepper
1-8 oz. jar Cheez Whiz
1-10 oz. pkg. frozen broccoli,
 thawed and drained
1 C. chopped tomato
¼ tsp. basil
1 T. butter, melted

Preheat oven to 350°. Combine beef, ¼ cup cracker crumbs, egg, onion and salt; mix lightly. Form into 12 meatballs; brown in oil. Combine rice and pepper; place in bottom of 1½-quart buttered casserole. Cover with meatballs. Combine Cheez Whiz, broccoli, tomato and basil. Pour over rice and meatballs. Top with remaining cracker crumbs tossed with butter. Bake at 350° for 30 minutes. Makes 4 to 6 servings.

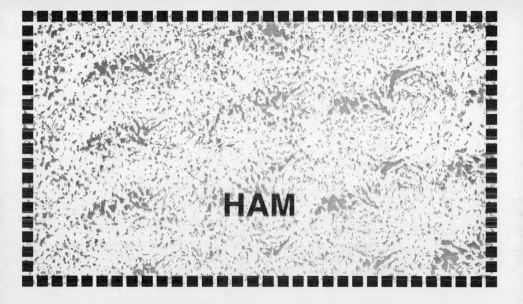

SCALLOPED HAM, POTATOES AND CARROTS

2 T. oil	1 C. milk
1 thin center slice smoked ham (¾ lb.)	3 C. sliced, pared potatoes
2¼ tsp. flour	1 C. sliced, scraped carrots
1 can cream of mushroom soup, undiluted	¼ C. minced onions
	Salt and pepper to taste

Preheat oven to 375°. In skillet, brown ham lightly on both sides; remove from skillet and cut into serving size pieces. Stir flour into fat left in skillet; add soup. Then slowly stir in milk. Heat, stirring until boiling. In 2-quart buttered casserole, arrange slices of ham, potatoes, carrots, onions until all are used; sprinkle vegetables lightly with salt and pepper. Pour on soup mixture. Bake, covered, 1 hour. Uncover; bake 15 minutes longer or until potatoes are fork-tender. Makes 3 to 4 servings.

HAM AND POTATO SCALLOP

1½ lbs. ham chunks
(6 to 8 slices)
8 to 10 medium potatoes,
peeled and sliced
2 medium onions, thinly
sliced

Salt and pepper to taste
1 C. grated Cheddar or
American cheese
1-10 oz. can cream of
mushroom soup
¼ tsp. paprika

Put half of ham, potatoes and onions in slow cooker. Sprinkle with salt, pepper and half of cheese. Repeat with remaining ham, potatoes, onions and cheese. Spoon soup over top. Sprinkle with paprika. Cover and cook 8 to 10 hours on low heat, or 4 to 5 hours on high heat.

MACARONI-HAM CASSEROLE

2 tsp. salt
4 oz. elbow macaroni
3 C. boiling water
1 T. oleo or butter
¼ C. chopped green pepper
¼ C. chopped onion
1 C. chopped ham

1-10½ oz. can cream of
  mushroom soup
½ C. milk
1 T. chopped pimento
1 T. parsley
⅛ tsp. pepper
½ C. grated American cheese

Preheat oven to 375°. Add salt and macaroni to boiling water. Boil rapidly; stir constantly for 2 minutes. Cover, remove from heat and let stand 10 minutes. Meanwhile, melt oleo in saucepan. Add green pepper and onion, simmer 5 minutes. Add diced ham and brown lightly. Rinse macaroni with warm water and drain. Combine ham mixture, mushroom soup, milk, pimento, parsley and pepper with macaroni. Put in 1½-quart greased casserole; sprinkle with cheese and bake 45 minutes. 55

HAM AND MAC BAKE

1 C. macaroni
¼ C. flour
2 T. prepared mustard
Dash of pepper
2 C. cubed cooked ham
1½ C. soft bread crumbs

¼ C. butter
2 T. brown sugar
¼ tsp. salt
2 C. milk
2 medium apples, peeled
  and sliced
2 T. butter, melted

Preheat oven to 350°. Cook macaroni in boiling water until tender; drain. In large saucepan, melt the ¼ cup oleo; blend in flour, brown sugar, mustard, salt and pepper. Add milk all at once and cook, stirring, until thickened and bubbly. Stir in cooked macaroni, ham, apple slices. Turn mixture into 2-quart casserole. Combine bread crumbs and 2 tablespoons butter and sprinkle on top of casserole. Bake, uncovered, 35 minutes. Makes 6 servings.

HAM ONE-DISH MEAL

3 C. thinly sliced potatoes
1 small onion, thinly sliced
1 C. thinly sliced carrots
2 C. diced, cooked ham

2 T. flour
1 can Cheddar cheese soup
½ C. milk
⅛ tsp. pepper

Preheat oven to 350°. Combine potatoes, onion, carrots and ham; place in 9x13" greased pan. Blend together the flour, soup, milk and pepper in a saucepan and cook, stirring constantly until the mixture boils. Pour over vegetables and ham. Cover and bake 1 hour. Remove lid and bake 30 minutes longer. Makes 8 to 10 servings.

HAM-VEGETABLE CASSEROLE

½ C. chopped onion
⅓ C. flour
1 T. prepared mustard
1½ tsp. Worcestershire sauce
1-16 oz. can tomatoes, cut up
4 C. cubed, fully cooked ham
3-10 oz. pkgs. frozen mixed vegetables, cooked and drained <u>or</u> 3-16 oz. cans mixed vegetables, drained

1½ C. bread crumbs
2 T. butter
¼ C. butter
½ tsp. salt
Dash of pepper
1-14½ oz. can evaporated milk

Preheat oven to 350°. In saucepan, cook onion in ¼ cup butter until tender, but not brown. Blend in flour, salt, pepper, mustard and Worcestershire sauce. Add tomatoes and milk. Cook and stir until thickened and bubbly. Remove from heat, stir in ham and vegetables. Put into greased 13x8¾x1¾" baking dish. Top with bread crumbs mixed with 2 tablespoons melted butter. Bake 30 minutes. Makes 12 servings.

HAM CASSEROLE

2 C. cubed, cooked ham
1 can undiluted mushroom
  soup
1 C. diced celery
1½ C. cooked rice
¾ C. mayonnaise
1 tsp. grated onion

1 T. lemon juice
3 hard-boiled eggs, sliced
½ tsp. salt
TOPPING:
½ C. slivered almonds
1 C. crushed cornflakes

Preheat oven to 350°. Mix all ingredients except topping and place in 7½x11" buttered pan. Top with almonds and cornflakes and bake 45 minutes. Makes 6 to 8 servings.

HAM AND NOODLES WITH PEAS

1½ C. medium wide noodles
3 T. butter
2 T. flour
1 C. grated process cheese
1 tsp. salt
2 T. catsup

1 T. horseradish
2 C. cooked ham, cut into cubes
2 C. canned peas, drained
¼ C. fresh bread crumbs, buttered

Preheat oven to 350°. Cook noodles according to directions; drain. Melt 2 tablespoons butter; add flour, stir until smooth. Gradually add milk; cook, stirring until smooth and thickened. Remove from heat; add cheese. Stir until melted; add noodles, salt, catsup, horseradish, ham and peas. Pour into 1½-quart buttered casserole. Top with buttered crumbs. Bake 30 minutes. Makes 4 servings.

POULTRY

SWEET AND SOUR CHICKEN DINNER

6 medium carrots, cut into
½" chunks
½ C. finely chopped green
pepper
½ C. finely chopped onion
3 chicken breasts, cut
lengthwise

½ tsp. salt
1-10 oz. jar sweet-sour
sauce
1-15¼ oz. can pineapple
chunks, drained
3 T. cornstarch
3 T. cold water
Hot cooked rice

In a crockery cooker, place carrots, green pepper and onion. Top with chicken breasts. Sprinkle with salt. Pour sweet-sour sauce and pineapple chunks over all; cover. Cook on low 7 to 8 hours or high 3½ to 4 hours. Remove chicken, keeping it warm. Blend cornstarch and water, stir into juices in crock pot. Cover; cook on high 10 to 15 minutes or until thickened. Season to taste and serve on rice. Makes 6 servings.

BAKED CHICKEN PUFF

1 can cream of mushroom
  soup, undiluted
⅓ C. milk
½ tsp. salt
1 C. diced, cooked chicken
  or turkey

2 C. cooked peas, green
  beans or broccoli
4 eggs, separated
⅓ C. grated Cheddar
  cheese

Preheat oven to 375°. Combine undiluted soup, milk and salt in 1½-quart buttered casserole. Add chicken and vegetables. Bake 10 minutes. Meanwhile, beat egg whites until stiff. Then with same beater, thoroughly beat egg yolks; add cheese. Lightly fold yolks into whites, and pile into chicken mixture. Bake 30 minutes. Makes 6 servings.

SCALLYWAGS CHICKEN-RICE CASSEROLE

1 qt. rich chicken broth	2 hard-boiled eggs, diced
1 C. rice	¼ C. chopped onion
2 C. cubed chicken, cooked	1 can cream of chicken soup
1 green pepper, diced	Salt and pepper to taste
3 T. butter	1½ C. buttered bread crumbs

Preheat oven to 350°. Cook rice in chicken broth until tender. <u>Do not drain.</u> Cook onions until transparent. Thin soup with cream until consistency of white sauce. Combine all ingredients except crumbs and put in buttered 2 quart casserole. Top with crumbs. Bake 30 to 45 minutes.

CHICKEN AND RICE CARIBBEAN

1-2½ lb. frying chicken
1 C. chopped onion
¼ C. chopped green pepper
1-8 oz. can tomato sauce
2 tsp. salt
1 C. ripe olives, cut up
1 pimento, cut in strips

3 T. oil
½ C. chopped celery
1½ C. raw rice
2 C. water
½ tsp. oregano
2 C. peas

Brown cut-up chicken in hot oil in Dutch oven or heavy type pan. Remove chicken. In Dutch oven, cook onion, celery, and green pepper for 5 minutes until tender, but not brown. Stir in raw rice, tomato sauce, water, salt and oregano. Heat to boiling and stir again. Add olives. Arrange browned chicken over rice and so forth. Cover. Cook over low heat about 40 minutes until chicken is tender. Top with peas and pimento, cooking long enough to heat through. Makes 6 servings.

CHICKEN RICE CASSEROLE

1 C. rice, precooked
1 chicken, cut up
1-10½ oz. can cream of
  chicken soup

1-10½ oz. can cream of
  mushroom soup
1 pkg. dry onion soup

Preheat oven to 350°. Place rice in bottom of 9x13" buttered casserole and then lay chicken pieces on that. Pour soups over chicken. Sprinkle dry onion soup on top. No salt needs to be added as the soups and dry onion mix is enough. Bake 1 hour or until chicken is done.

CRISP NOODLE CHICKEN

1 broiler-fryer chicken,
  cut up
1-10½ oz. can cream of
  chicken soup

1 C. dairy sour cream
3 T. onion soup mix
⅛ tsp. pepper
1-3 oz. can chow mein
  noodles

Preheat oven to 375°. Place chicken in a single layer in a 1½-quart casserole. In a bowl, combine soup, sour cream, soup mix and pepper; blend thoroughly. Spread over chicken, sprinkle with noodles. Bake 1 hour or until chicken is tender. Makes 4 servings.

CHICKEN AND NOODLE CASSEROLE

1-6 oz. pkg. noodles, cooked
2 C. diced chicken, cooked
1 C. mushrooms, sliced
¼ C. grated cheese
1 pimento, chopped

2 C. milk
1 C. chicken broth
5 T. flour
5 T. margarine
1 T. buttered crumbs

Preheat oven to 350°. Make sauce of margarine, flour, broth and milk. Add cheese, stir until melted. Add noodles, chicken, mushrooms and pimento to the sauce and stir until mixed. Place in greased 2-quart casserole and put on buttered crumbs and bake 30 minutes.

CHICKEN CASSEROLE

2 C. chicken, cooked and
  cubed
1 can cream of chicken soup
1 can cream of mushroom
  soup

2 C. uncooked macaroni
2 C. milk
½ lb. American cheese,
  diced
2 medium onions or onion
  flakes

Preheat oven to 350°. Combine all of these ingredients and let stand overnight in buttered 2½-quart size casserole. Sprinkle with paprika and bake 1 hour. Serves 8 to 10.

CHINESE CHICKEN WITH VEGETABLES

2 whole chicken breasts,
  split, skinned and boned
3 T. cooking oil
1 lb. mushrooms, sliced
2 medium onions, sliced and
  separated into rings
1 C. bias-cut celery
2 cloves garlic, minced
¾ tsp. ground ginger

½ C. water
¼ C. soy sauce
2-6 oz. pkgs. frozen pea
  pods, partially thawed
2 T. cornstarch
2 T. water
Hot cooked rice
½ C. chopped walnuts

Cut chicken in 2x¼" strips. Cook in hot oil 5 minutes, stirring constantly. Add mushrooms, onion, celery, garlic, ginger, ½ cup water and soy sauce. Cook until boiling, reduce heat to low. Cover and simmer 5 minutes. Increase heat to medium. Stir in pea pods. Return to boil. Cover and cook 3 minutes. Dissolve cornstarch in water, stir into chicken mixture. Cook and stir. Serve over hot rice. Garnish with walnuts. Serves 6.

CHICKEN IN HONEY SAUCE

3 whole chicken breasts,
  split
¼ tsp. pepper
1-20 oz. can pineapple
  chunks in juice
⅓ C. chopped onion
½ C. cider vinegar
¼ C. cornstarch
1 T. soy sauce
1-6 oz. pkg. frozen pea
  pods, thawed

1 tsp. salt
2 T. oil
2 C. bias-cut carrots
1 C. water
⅓ C. honey
2 chicken bouillon cubes
½ C. water
Hot cooked rice

Season chicken breasts with salt and pepper. Heat oil in 12" skillet over medium heat. Meanwhile, drain pineapple, reserving juice. Brown chicken in oil about 10 minutes. Stir in carrots, onion, water, vinegar, honey, soy sauce, chicken cubes and reserved pineapple juice. Cover; simmer 35 minutes or until chicken is tender. Remove chicken. Stir together cornstarch and ½ cup water. Stir cornstarch mixture into pan juices. Cook, stirring constantly, until mixture boils, about 2 minutes. Stir in pea pods and pineapple. Cook 1 minute. Arrange chicken and vegetables on hot rice. Stove top - 55 minutes. Makes 6 servings.

TURKEY TETRAZZINI

¾ lb. mushrooms, sliced
1 small green pepper, slivered
¼ C. butter
3 T. flour
2 tsp. salt
¼ tsp. pepper
2½ C. light cream

4 C. diced turkey
2 pimentos, chopped
2 T. sherry
6 oz. fine spaghetti, cooked
2 egg yolks, beaten
Grated Parmesan cheese

Preheat oven to 300°. Cook mushrooms and peppers in butter 5 minutes. Blend in flour and seasonings. Add cream and cook, stirring, until thickened. Add next 3 ingredients and heat. Put spaghetti into greased shallow baking dish. Add small amount of turkey mixture to egg yolks, then return, stirring, to turkey mixture. Bake in slow 300° oven 45 minutes. Put under broiler to brown lightly. Makes 6 servings.

TURKETTI CASSEROLE

1¼ C. spaghetti, broken into 2" pieces
1½ to 2 C. cut-up cooked turkey
¼ C. diced pimentos
¼ C. chopped green pepper
½ C. chopped onion

1 can cream of mushroom soup
½ C. turkey broth <u>or</u> water
⅛ tsp. pepper
1¾ C. grated sharp Cheddar cheese

Preheat oven to 350°. Cook spaghetti as package directs; drain. Place turkey, pimentos, green pepper, and onion in 1½-quart buttered casserole. Pour in mushroom soup and broth; add salt, pepper, 1¼ cups grated cheese and spaghetti. With 2 forks, lightly toss until all is well mixed and coated with sauce. Sprinkle remaining ½ cup cheese on top and bake 45 minutes. Makes 4 servings.

HOLIDAY TURKEY CASSEROLE

6 T. butter
1½ C. diagonally sliced
  celery
1 medium onion, minced
6 T. flour
1 tsp. salt
Dash of pepper
3 C. milk
1 can cream of mushroom
  soup, undiluted

2 C. cubed, cooked ham
2 C. cubed, cooked turkey
2 T. minced pimento
¼ tsp. dried basil
3 T. cooking sherry
½ C. grated sharp Cheddar
  cheese
Parsley sprigs

Preheat oven to 350°. In butter, in large saucepan, saute celery and onion until tender. Stir in flour, salt, pepper; add milk. Cook, stirring constantly, until mixture thickens. Add soup, ham, turkey, pimento, basil, sherry. Taste, add more seasonings if needed. Put in 2-quart buttered casserole; top with cheese. Bake, uncovered, 1 hour. Garnish with parsley. Makes 8 servings.

NOTES • NOTES • NOTES • NOTES • NOTES

TUNA & SEAFOOD

CHINESE TUNA CASSEROLE

7 oz. can chunk-style tuna,
  drained and flaked
3 oz. can chow mein noodles
1 C. chopped celery
¼ C. chopped onion

¼ C. chopped green
  pepper
½ C. broken cashew nuts
10½ oz. can cream of
  mushroom soup
⅔ C. water
⅔ C. crushed potato chips

Preheat oven to 350°. Combine tuna with noodles, celery, onion, green pepper, and nuts. Stir together soup and water; pour over tuna mixture. Stir slightly. Place in 1½-quart casserole; sprinkle with potato chips. Bake 35 to 40 minutes.

EXCELLENT TUNA CASSEROLE

2 C. noodles, cooked
2 C. tuna
1 C. sour cream
1 C. cottage cheese
1 can mushroom soup
1 small jar pimento
1 T. grated onion

¼ tsp. Tabasco sauce
1-6 oz. can mushrooms and juice
1 tsp. Worcestershire sauce
¼ C. chopped green pepper
½ C. salted cashews
Chinese noodles

Preheat oven to 325°. Mix all ingredients together and put in 9x13" buttered pan. Top with Chinese noodles. Bake 35 minutes. Makes 6 to 8 servings.

TUNA NOODLE CASSEROLE

1 pkg. noodles, cooked
1 pkg. mixed vegetables,
  cooked

1 can of mushroom soup
1-10½ oz. can of milk
2 small cans tuna fish

Preheat oven to 350°. Cook noodles and vegetables according to package directions. Add the soup, milk and tuna and bake 45 minutes in 1½-quart greased casserole. Buttered crackers or bread cubes may be put on as a topping before baking, if desired.

BUFFET PARTY CASSEROLE

1-8 oz. pkg. fine noodles
¼ C. oil
2-7 oz. cans tuna
2-4 oz. cans mushrooms
1 peeled garlic clove (whole)
1 minced small onion
1 T. flour

1 tsp. Worcestershire sauce
1 can cream of chicken
  soup, undiluted
¼ C. sherry
1-5 oz. can shrimp
½ C. Parmesan cheese

Preheat oven to 350°. Cook noodles in boiling salted water as directed on package. Drain. Meanwhile, put oil and oil from tuna into a skillet. Drain mushrooms, saving liquid, and put them into skillet; add garlic and onion. Cook, stirring until onion is tender, but not brown. Remove garlic. Blend in flour, stir in mushroom liquid and Worcestershire sauce. Cook until thickened, stirring. Stir in wine and soup. Break tuna into bite-size pieces and add with shrimp and noodles to sauce. Put in 3-quart buttered casserole and sprinkle with cheese. Bake 40 minutes. Makes 12 servings.

CRAB AND SHRIMP CASSEROLE

1 can crabmeat
1 can cooked shrimp
2 cans mushroom soup
1 C. finely sliced celery
½ C. minced onion

⅓ C. chopped green pepper
1-3 oz. can chow mein
 noodles
¼ C. slivered almonds
1 C. crushed potato chips

Preheat oven to 375°. Combine all ingredients except potato chips and put in 1½-quart buttered casserole. Top with chips and bake 30 minutes.

DOUBLE SHRIMP CASSEROLE

3 C. cooked noodles (1½ C., uncooked)
¾ C. milk
¼ C. diced celery
¼ tsp. salt
1 C. cooked shrimp or 1 can shrimp

½ C. chow mein noodles
1 can frozen shrimp soup
½ C. mayonnaise
1 T. chopped onion
⅓ C. shredded Cheddar cheese

Preheat oven to 350°. Cook noodles in water and drain. Thaw soup; combine with milk, mayonnaise, celery, onion and salt; mix well. Pour into 1½-quart buttered casserole. Bake at 350° for 30 to 35 minutes. Top with chow mein noodles and bake 10 minutes more. Makes 4 to 6 servings.

SHRIMPALAYA CASSEROLE

6 oz. elbow macaroni
   (1½ C.)
2 strips bacon, diced
½ C. minced onion
½ C. minced green pepper
½ clove garlic, minced
1-#2 can tomatoes (2½ C.)
1 tsp. salt

½ lb. cubed, cooked ham <u>or</u>
   canned luncheon meat
   (about 1¼ C.)
1 C. cooked, cleaned shrimp
½ C. day-old bread crumbs
2 T. Parmesan cheese
2 T. melted butter

Preheat oven to 350°. Cook macaroni in boiling water until tender; drain. Meanwhile, saute bacon until crisp in skillet. Add onions, green pepper and garlic; saute until tender. Add tomatoes and salt; heat. Add macaroni, ham and shrimp. Pour into 1½-quart buttered casserole. Combine bread crumbs, cheese and butter; sprinkle on top of casserole. Bake until hot and bubbly; about 1 hour. Makes 4 servings.

SALMON-OLIVE CASSEROLE

1-5 oz. pkg. rice (1⅓ C.)
½ C. milk
½ lb. Cheddar cheese,
 thinly sliced

¾ tsp. salt
Dash of pepper
1-7¾ oz. can salmon,
 flaked
¼ C. chopped, stuffed olives

Preheat oven to 350°. Cook rice as package directs. Meanwhile, combine milk, cheese, salt, and pepper in double boiler. Heat, stirring occasionally, until well-blended and smooth. In 1½-quart buttered casserole, alternate layers of cooked rice, salmon, olives and cheese sauce, ending with sauce. Garnish with stuffed olives. Bake 30 minutes. Makes 6 servings.

SALMON-CAULIFLOWER CASSEROLE

1-10 oz. pkg. frozen
  cauliflower
¼ C. finely chopped onions
1 T. butter
1-10½ oz. can Cheddar
  cheese soup
1-4 oz. can chopped
  mushrooms, drained

¼ C. grated Parmesan
  cheese
1 T. lemon juice
½ tsp. dried dill weed
Dash of pepper
1-7¾ oz. can salmon,
  drained, bones removed
  and broken into pieces
Lemon twist
Parsley

Preheat oven to 350°. In saucepan, cook cauliflower in a small amount of salted water 3 minutes. Drain; cut cauliflower into small pieces. Set aside. In saucepan, cook onion in butter until tender. Stir in cheese soup and heat through. Stir in mushrooms, Parmesan cheese, lemon juice, dill weed and pepper. Fold in salmon and cauliflower. Put mixture into 1-quart ungreased casserole. Bake, uncovered, 30 to 35 minutes. Garnish with lemon twist and parsley. Makes 4 servings.

FISH STICKS POLYNESIAN

⅓ C. sugar
1-13¾ oz. can pineapple
  tidbits
1 vegetable bouillon cube
2 T. vinegar
1-10 oz. pkg. frozen peas,
  thawed

2 T. cornstarch
2 tsp. soy sauce
¼ tsp. salt
1½ C. cooked rice
1-8 oz. pkg. frozen, fried,
  breaded fish sticks
Carrot curls

Preheat oven to 350°. In medium saucepan, combine sugar and cornstarch. Drain pineapple tidbits, reserving ⅔ cup syrup. Gradually stir syrup into sugar mixture. Add soy sauce, vegetable bouillon cube and salt. Cook, stirring constantly, until thickened and bubbly. Remove from heat; stir in vinegar. Combine cooked rice, thawed peas and pineapple tidbits. Stir sauce into rice mixture. Put into greased 1-quart casserole. Arrange fish sticks spoke-fashion atop rice mixture. Bake 25 to 30 minutes. Then top with carrot curls. Makes 4 servings.

AFTER-FIVE CASSEROLE

2 T. chopped onion
1 T. butter
1-10½ oz. can cream of
  celery soup
½ C. shredded Cheddar
  cheese

2 C. cooked, diced potatoes
1 C. cooked, cut green beans
1 T. diced pimento
1-7¾ oz. can salmon,
  drained
2 T. buttered bread crumbs

Preheat oven to 400°. Cook onion in butter until tender. Blend in soup, milk and cheese. Heat until cheese melts; stir often. Add potatoes, green beans and pimento. Pour ⅓ of the mixture into 1-quart greased casserole. With a fork, break salmon into chunks; place half of salmon on top of potato mixture. Repeat layers. Top with remaining potato mixture; sprinkle crumbs on top. Garnish with chopped parsley, if desired. Bake 20 minutes. Makes 4 servings.

VEGETABLES

CARROT CASSEROLE

5 C. sliced carrots
2 large onions, diced

⅓ C. margarine
½ lb. Velveeta, sliced

Preheat oven to 350°. Cook carrots until almost tender. Saute onion in margarine. Layer carrots in 2-quart buttered casserole alternately with sliced Velveeta. Pour onions and margarine over carrots. Bake 30 minutes.

POLKA-DOT BAKED MACARONI

2 C. cooked macaroni
 (½ lb.)
¼ C. butter
¼ C. flour
1 can cream of chicken
 soup, undiluted
1 C. milk

1½ C. grated sharp Cheddar
 cheese
1 pkg. frozen peas and
 carrots, thawed
1 T. butter
⅛ tsp. salt
1 T. water

Preheat oven to 400°. Cook ½ pound macaroni as label directs; drain. Meanwhile, in saucepan, melt ¼ cup butter; stir in flour and then soup and milk; cook, stirring until smooth and thickened. Combine macaroni, soup mixture, ¾ cup cheese, and ½ package of peas and carrots. Turn into 2-quart greased casserole, sprinkle rest of cheese on top. Place other ½ package of peas and carrots in a small casserole with 1 tablespoon butter, salt and water. Bake small casserole, covered, macaroni casserole, uncovered, 30 minutes. When done, spoon the ½ package of peas and carrots around casserole to make a colorful wreath. Makes 6 to 8 servings.

EASY CASSEROLE

2 cans corned beef hash
2 cans mixed vegetables,
   drained

1 pkg. tater tots
1 can onion rings

Preheat oven to 350°. Line sides and bottom of 10x10x1" buttered casserole with hash. Put vegetables in center and top with tater tots and onion rings. Bake 1 hour.

VEGETABLE CASSEROLE

1 pkg. frozen cauliflower
1 can green beans, drained
½ C. chopped onion
½ C. chopped celery
½ tsp. salt

½ C. butter
1 C. seasoned croutons
2 cans mushroom soup
½ C. shredded Cheddar
  cheese

Preheat oven to 350 to 375°. Cook cauliflower until tender and drain. Combine all ingredients except cheese and butter; put in large 2-quart buttered casserole; sprinkle with cheese and dot with butter. Bake 35 minutes.

ELEGANT VEGETABLE CASSEROLE

2-10 oz. pkgs. frozen
  chopped or whole
  broccoli
2-10 oz. pkgs. frozen
  cauliflower

1 can cream of chicken soup
1 can Cheddar cheese soup
¼ C. whole milk
1 C. buttered bread crumbs
1 can onion rings

Preheat oven to 350°. Cook vegetables according to directions and drain. Mix soups and milk. Place vegetables in 9x13" pan. Pour soup mixture over vegetables. Top with crumbs. Sprinkle broken onion rings over top of crumbs. Bake, uncovered, 30 to 45 minutes.

VEGETABLE CASSEROLE

1 pkg. frozen green beans
1 pkg. frozen lima beans
1 pkg. frozen peas
1⅓ C. mayonnaise
1 T. Worcestershire

¼ tsp. Tabasco
1 medium onion, grated
½ T. lemon juice
1 T. prepared mustard
1 can water chestnuts,
  sliced

Preheat oven to 350°. Cook packages of vegetables separately, according to directions and drain. Mix with water chestnuts and put in 10x14" buttered casserole. Blend remaining ingredients and pour over vegetables. Sprinkle crushed potato chips on top if desired. Bake 30 minutes. Makes 4 to 6 servings.

ORIENTAL STIR-FRIED VEGETABLES

1½ lbs. fresh broccoli
4 T. oil
1 C. chicken broth
1-16 oz. can bean sprouts, drained
1-8 oz. can water chestnuts, drained and sliced
¼ lb. fresh mushrooms, sliced

½ tsp. salt
1 clove garlic, minced
1-6 oz. pkg. frozen pea pods, thawed
2 T. cornstarch
1 tsp. sugar
1 T. soy sauce
⅛ tsp. ginger
1 T. toasted sesame seeds

Remove flowerets from broccoli and cut in half. Cut stalks into 2x¼" strips. Heat oil in 12" skillet over medium heat. Add broccoli and stir-fry 1 minute. Add salt, garlic and ½ cup of the chicken broth. Cover and cook 3 minutes. Uncover, stir-fry 3 minutes. Add sprouts, chestnuts, mushrooms, and pea pods; stir-fry 2 minutes. Combine cornstarch, sugar, ginger, soy sauce and remaining ½ cup chicken broth. Stir to blend. Stir cornstarch into skillet. Cook until it boils, stirring constantly. Cook 1 more minute. Sprinkle with sesame seeds. Cooking time - 16 minutes. Makes 6 servings.

CURRIED BAKED CAULIFLOWER

1 large head cauliflower
½ tsp. salt
1 can cream of chicken soup
1-4 oz. pkg. shredded
  Cheddar cheese

⅓ C. mayonnaise
¼ tsp. curry powder
¼ C. dry bread crumbs
2 T. butter, melted

Preheat oven to 350°. Cook broken cauliflower in water with ½ teaspoon salt. Drain well. Stir together undiluted soup, cheese, mayonnaise, and curry powder. Add cauliflower; mix well. Put in 2-quart buttered casserole. Toss bread crumbs with butter, sprinkle on top. Bake 30 minutes.

BROCCOLI CASSEROLE

1 stick oleo
¾ C. chopped celery
1 medium chopped onion
1 can cream of mushroom soup
1 can cream of chicken soup

½ soup can milk
1 lb. Velveeta cheese, sliced
2½ C. cooked rice
2-22 oz. pkgs. frozen chopped broccoli, thawed
1 can diced water chestnuts

Preheat oven to 325°. In deep saucepan, melt oleo and add celery and onion. Saute. Add soups and milk. Mix thoroughly. Add sliced Velveeta to mixture. Mix until smooth and creamy. Add rice and mix well. Add broccoli (not cooked) just so it isn't frozen. <u>Important:</u> Be sure broccoli doesn't have too much liquid in it. Add water chestnuts. Mix until creamy. Put in large 9x13" buttered casserole. Bake, uncovered, 50 minutes. Makes 16 to 20 servings.

CHEESEY BROCCOLI BAKE

1-10 oz. pkg. frozen
  broccoli, chopped
1-10¾ oz. can Cheddar
  cheese soup

1 small can ham, chicken or
  turkey, flaked
1 C. cooked rice
½ C. dairy sour cream
½ C. buttered bread crumbs

Preheat oven to 350°. Cook broccoli until barely tender. Drain well. Stir soup and sour cream together. Add remaining ingredients to soup and sour cream mixture (except bread crumbs). Sprinkle with bread crumbs and bake 30 to 35 minutes in 1½-quart casserole. Makes 4 to 6 servings.

ASPARAGUS CASSEROLE

1 bunch fresh asparagus or 1 can	⅓ tsp. pepper
1 C. soft bread crumbs	2 T. flour
⅓ C. dried buttered crumbs	4 hard-boiled eggs, chopped
2 C. milk	1 tsp. salt
¼ C. grated cheese	3 T. butter

Preheat oven to 350°. Cut asparagus in 1" pieces, cook until tender; drain. Make a sauce of butter, flour, seasonings and bread crumbs. Put a layer of asparagus in bottom of 1-quart buttered casserole. Add sauce and half of hard-boiled eggs. Repeat with additional layer. Sprinkle with dried buttered crumbs mixed with the cheese. Bake 20 minutes. Makes 4 servings.

ESCALLOPED CORN

1 pint can corn	1 tsp. sugar
1 tsp. salt	¾ C. crushed cracker
Dash of pepper	crumbs
3 T. melted butter	2 eggs, well beaten
	1¼ C. milk

Preheat oven to 350°. Mix all together and put in 1½-quart buttered casserole. Bake 1 hour.

CELERY CASSEROLE

4 C. coarsely diced celery	1 tsp. salt
4 T. butter	1¼ C. light cream
1½ T. flour	½ C. slivered almonds
⅛ tsp. white pepper	4 oz. cream cheese

Preheat oven to 325°. Cook celery in salted water 5 to 8 minutes, then drain. Put in 1½-quart buttered baking dish. Cover with white sauce made in skillet by blending the butter and flour, then stirring in cream and seasonings with the cheese. Dot with slivered almonds and sprinkle with a little paprika. Bake 25 minutes. Makes 6 to 8 servings.

BEANS-BOSTON BAKED

1 qt. dried navy beans
  (about 2 lbs.)
2 tsp. salt
½ lb. salt pork, cut in
  pieces

3 small onions, sliced
⅔ C. brown sugar, packed
2 tsp. salt
2 tsp. dry mustard
⅔ C. molasses

Preheat oven to 350°. Cover beans with 3 quarts water; let stand 12 to 18 hours in a cool place. Add 2 teaspoons salt to beans and soaking water; bring to boil. Cover and simmer until skins start to crack. Drain (reserve liquid). Put beans in baking dish. Add pork and onion. Combine remaining ingredients. Add 4 cups reserved bean liquid. Pour onto beans. Stir slightly. Cover and bake at 350°, 3½ hours. Add water, if necessary. Beans should be soupy. Pack into hot jars, leaving 1" head space room. Adjust caps. Process pints 1 hour and 20 minutes; quarts 1 hour and 35 minutes at 10 pounds pressure. Yields: 6 pints.

GOLDEN-TOPPED BAKED BEANS

2-1 lb. cans baked beans
 in tomato sauce
1 T. minced onion
1 tsp. prepared mustard
1 tsp. horseradish
Prepared mustard

8-¼" thick slices Canadian
 bacon
4-¼" thick orange slices,
 halved
¼ C. brown sugar
1 T. butter
Whole cloves

Preheat oven to 400°. In deep fluted 9" pie plate (buttered) or shallow casserole (5-cup capacity), combine beans, minced onion, 1 teaspoon mustard and horseradish. Spread a bit of mustard on each slice of Canadian bacon; on top of beans, arrange bacon with orange slices, pinwheel fashion. Sprinkle all with brown sugar; dot with butter; stud with whole cloves. Bake 25 minutes. Makes 4 servings.

CREAMY MACARONI AND GREEN BEANS

Preheat oven to 375°. Boil 1½ cups macaroni, 3 cups water and ½ teaspoon salt 8 minutes. Cook macaroni according to directions and drain. Put into 2-quart greased casserole and cover and mix lightly with following White Sauce: Add 3 tablespoons flour to a small amount of milk and make a smooth thickening. Add 3 tablespoons shortening, ¾ teaspoon salt, ¼ teaspoon pepper, and remaining milk to equal a total of 2 cups. Cook until smooth. Then add 2 tablespoons chopped onion and ½ cup diced cheese, blend until the cheese melts. Now, add 2 cups cooked, drained green beans. Put into casserole and bake 30 minutes.

IOWA SUCCOTASH

1-12 oz. Mexican style
   whole kernel corn
1½ C. drained, cooked
   frozen or canned
   beans

1 C. light cream
1 tsp. sugar
1 tsp. salt
⅛ tsp. pepper
⅛ tsp. paprika

Preheat oven to 350°. In 1½-quart greased casserole, mix together all the ingredients. Bake 30 minutes, covered, in greased casserole.

DIFFERENT HOMINY CASSEROLE

2 eggs
1½ C. milk
1-1 lb. 13 oz. can hominy,
  drained

½ C. corn meal
2 tsp. salt
Dash of pepper
3 T. butter

Preheat oven to 325°. In 1½-quart buttered casserole, beat eggs lightly; add milk; then add hominy, corn meal, salt and pepper; dot with butter. Bake 45 minutes or until mixture is set. Makes 5 servings.

SQUASH CASSEROLE

2 to 3 C. yellow or zucchini
  squash, cooked
1 C. diced celery
1 C. diced onion
½ lb. pork sausage
2 beaten eggs

1 C. cracker crumbs
½ C. cubed Cheddar
  cheese
½ tsp. salt
¼ tsp. thyme
Parmesan cheese

Preheat oven to 350°. Lightly fry sausage to remove grease; saute celery and onion with sausage. Mix eggs, crumbs, cheese, salt and thyme. Mix into squash with sausage mixture. Bake at 350° for 35 minutes. Sprinkle with Parmesan cheese the last 10 minutes of baking. Use 2-quart greased dish.

GREEN AND GOLD CASSEROLE

1-6 oz. pkg. hash brown
  potatoes with onions
1-10 oz. pkg. frozen peas
2 C. sliced celery
1½ C. water
2 T. butter

¾ tsp. salt
⅛ tsp. pepper
1-10½ oz. can condensed
  cream of shrimp soup
⅔ C. milk
½ C. shredded Cheddar
  cheese

Preheat oven to 350°. In saucepan, combine dry potatoes, peas, celery, water, butter, salt andpepper. Bring to boiling; reduce heat and simmer, uncovered, until liquid is absorbed; about 5 minutes. Stir soup into milk; fold into potato mixture. Turn into ungreased 1½-quart casserole. Bake, uncovered, in 350° oven, 30 to 35 minutes. Sprinkle with cheese and bake 2 to 3 more minutes until cheese melts. Makes 8 servings.

GOLDEN POTATO BAKE

2 lbs. potatoes, peeled
  (about 6 medium potatoes)
1-16 oz. can diced carrots,
  drained _or_ 2 C. diced
  carrots, cooked and
  drained

Hot milk
2 T. butter
Salt to taste

Preheat oven to 350°. Cook potatoes in boiling, salted water until tender, drain. Add carrots. Mash at low speed with electric mixer; slowly beat in enough milk to make light and fluffy. Stir in the butter and a little salt and pepper. Put into greased 2-quart casserole and dot with butter, if desired. Bake 25 minutes. Makes 8 servings.

BASIL-SCALLOPED POTATOES

¼ C. butter
1 tsp. salt
⅛ tsp. pepper
½ C. snipped parsley
½ C. soft bread crumbs
¼ C. parsley, snipped

1 T. flour
1 tsp. dried basil, crushed
2 C. milk
6 to 8 medium potatoes,
 peeled and sliced
1 T. melted butter

Preheat oven to 325°. In a small saucepan, melt ¼ cup butter; stir in flour, salt, basil and pepper. Stir in the milk all at once. Cook and stir over medium heat until mixture thickens and bubbles. Stir in ½ cup parsley. Grease an 8x8x2" baking dish. Combine the potatoes and hot sauce; pour into greased dish. Cover; bake for 1 hour. Uncover; sprinkle center with bread crumbs, melted butter and ¼ cup parsley. Bake 30 to 45 minutes longer or until potatoes are fork-tender. Let stand 15 minutes before serving. Makes 6 servings.

EGG, CHEESE AND TOMATO CASSEROLE

6 C. diced French or Italian
  bread
1½ C. coarsely grated sharp
  Cheddar cheese
4 large eggs
2½ C. milk

⅛ tsp. nutmeg
1½ tsp. lightly salted butter
2 medium-sized tomatoes,
  sliced thin
¼ tsp. paprika

Preheat oven to 350°. In a large bowl, mix bread and 1¼ cups of the cheese. In a medium-sized bowl, beat eggs with milk and nutmeg. Pour over bread mixture and toss to mix. Let stand 15 to 30 minutes. Then spread about 3 cups of the bread mixture into a 3-quart oblong baking dish, cover with half of the tomatoes and then remaining bread mixture. Top with remaining tomato slices, sprinkle with remaining ¼ cup cheese. Bake until cheese is melted and a knife inserted in the center comes out clean; 40 to 45 minutes. Makes 4 servings.

CHEESE-TOMATO BAKE

4 medium tomatoes, peeled
1 tsp. sugar
Dash of pepper
8 oz. sharp process American
  cheese, shredded (2 C.)

½ C. finely chopped celery
¼ C. finely chopped onion
1 C. soft bread crumbs
2 T. butter, melted

Preheat oven to 350°. Slice tomatoes into fourths. Sprinkle with sugar and pepper. In bowl, toss together cheese, celery and onion. Place half of the tomato slices into greased 10x6x1¾" baking dish. Sprinkle on half of the cheese mixture over tomato slices. Repeat layers. Toss crumbs with butter; sprinkle over casserole mixture. Bake 25 to 30 minutes. Makes 6 servings.

BERMUDA CASSEROLE

4 Bermuda onions, cut in
  ¼" slices
6 slices day-old bread
1 C. finely crumbled blue
  cheese
1 C. undiluted evaporated
  milk or light cream

3 eggs, beaten
Salt
Hot pepper sauce
Butter
Paprika

Preheat oven to 375°. Parboil onion slices in boiling water 10 minutes. Trim crusts from bread and cut bread in small pieces. Butter 1½-quart baking dish. Put onion in dish and cover with bread squares. Sprinkle with cheese. Mix milk and eggs and season with salt and hot pepper sauce. Pour over ingredients in baking dish. Dot with butter and sprinkle lightly with paprika. Bake 40 minutes. Makes 6 servings.

SPINACH AND SPAGHETTI

1-10 oz. pkg. frozen
  chopped spinach
1 beaten egg
½ C. dairy sour cream
¼ C. milk
2 T. grated Parmesan cheese
2 tsp. minced dried onion

½ tsp. salt
Dash pepper
2 C. shredded Monterey
  Jack cheese
4 oz. spaghetti, cooked and
  drained
2 T. grated Parmesan
  cheese

Preheat oven to 350°. Cook spinach according to package directions; drain well. Combine beaten egg, dairy sour cream, milk, 2 tablespoons Parmesan cheese, onion, salt and pepper. Add the Monterey Jack cheese and mix well. Add the drained spinach and drained spaghetti; mix well again. Turn into 10x6x2" ungreased dish and sprinkle with remaining 2 tablespoons Parmesan cheese. Bake, covered, 15 minutes. Uncover, bake 20 minutes more or until heated through. Makes 4 servings.

NOTES • NOTES • NOTES • NOTES • NOTES

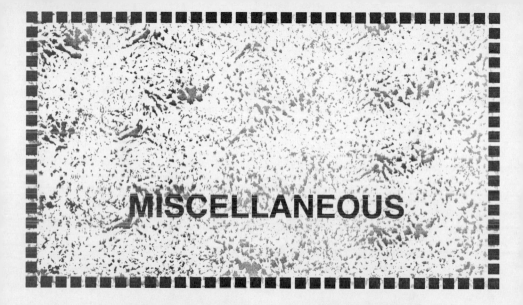

MISCELLANEOUS

DRIED BEEF CASSEROLE

½ lb. noodles, cook and drain
1-10½ oz. can cream of
  mushroom soup
1 C. milk

1-¼ lb. pkg. dried beef,
  cut up
1 C. peas
½ C. grated cheese

Preheat oven to 325°. Cook and drain noodles. Combine soup and milk and heat through. Add to noodles, then stir in dried beef, peas and cheese. Bake 20 to 25 minutes in 2-quart greased dish.

CORNED BEEF CASSEROLE

7 oz. shell macaroni
1-12 oz. can corned beef, diced
2 C. diced Cheddar cheese

1-10½ oz. can cream of chicken soup
1 C. milk
½ C. chopped onion
2 slices bread, cubed
2 T. butter, melted

Preheat oven to 350°. Cook macaroni according to package directions; drain. Combine macaroni, corned beef, cheese, soup, milk and onion; blend. Turn into a 2-quart buttered casserole. Trim crusts from bread and cube; toss in butter. Arrange around edge of casserole. Bake 45 minutes and let stand 10 minutes before serving. Makes 8 to 10 servings.

MEAL-IN-A-CASSEROLE

1-24 oz. can corned beef hash
1-12 or 16 oz. can whole
  kernel corn, drained
1-10½ oz. can cream of
  chicken soup

1 small onion, chopped
1 T. parsley
½ C. grated cheese

Preheat oven to 350°. Line corned beef into greased pie plate and form into a nest. Combine corn, soup, chopped onion and parsley. Pour into nest. Top with cheese and bake 35 to 40 minutes. Makes 6 servings.

131

SAVORY BEEF CASSEROLE

2 lbs. stewing beef, cut
  into 1" cubes
¼ C. oil
1½ C. chopped onion
1-1 lb. can tomatoes
3 T. Minute tapioca
1-10½ oz. can condensed
  beef broth
1 clove garlic, minced

1 T. parsley flakes
2½ tsp. salt
¼ tsp. pepper
1 bay leaf
6 medium carrots, cut in
  strips
3 medium potatoes, cut in
  large cubes
½ C. sliced celery

Preheat oven to 350°. Brown beef cubes on all sides in hot oil in a large skillet. Add onion, tomatoes, tapioca, beef broth, garlic, parsley, salt, pepper and bay leaf. Bring mixture to boil. Turn into a 3-quart buttered casserole. Cover. Bake at 350° for 1 hour and 30 minutes or until meat is tender. Add carrots, potatoes and celery. Continue baking, covered for 1 hour or until vegetables are tender. Makes 6 to 8 servings.

CHOW MEIN

2 lb. beef roast or round
 steak, cubed or diced
3 T. oil
5 C. diced celery
8 small onions

1 large can Chinese
 vegetables
1 large can bean sprouts
2 T. cornstarch
3 T. soy sauce
Rice or chow mein noodles

Cut meat in cubes and sear 10 minutes in 3 tablespoons oil. Cover with 2 cups water and add celery and onions in kettle. Bring to a boil and simmer 1½ hours. Add Chinese vegetables and bean sprouts. Thicken with cornstarch and soy sauce. Serve over rice or chow mein noodles.

KANSAS CITY CASSEROLE

2½ to 3 lb. lean beef short
   ribs
2 tsp. salt
⅛ tsp. pepper
1 medium onion, sliced
1 T. chopped parsley

½ C. diced celery
2 medium potatoes,
   quartered
2 T. prepared horseradish
2-8 oz. or 1-15 oz. can
   tomato sauce with tomato
   bits

Preheat oven to 400°. Cut beef into serving-size pieces; sprinkle with salt and pepper, place in casserole. Brown meat, uncovered, in 400° oven for 1 hour. Add remaining ingredients and bake at 375°, 1 more hour. Makes 4 to 5 servings.

RIB-AND-BEAN BARBECUE CASSEROLE

4 lbs. spareribs, cut in
  2-rib pieces
⅓ C. soy sauce
3 T. honey
½ tsp. salt
4 medium onions, sliced
1 C. cut-up celery leaves
2 T. oil

2 dashes liquid hot pepper
  seasoning
½ tsp. thyme
¼ tsp. salt
¼ tsp. pepper
2-1 lb. 2 oz. cans baked
  beans, Boston style

Preheat oven to 350°. Place spareribs in 3-quart buttered casserole. Mix soy sauce, honey, ½ teaspoon salt; brush some over spareribs. Bake, covered, 2 hours. Meanwhile, saute onions and celery leaves in oil 5 minutes. Add pepper, seasoning, thyme, ¼ teaspoon salt, pepper, beans. At end of 2 hours, remove spareribs; skim surface fat from drippings; add bean mixture to casserole; top with spareribs. Brush surface of spareribs with some of the sauce. Bake 30 minutes longer. Makes 8 servings.

POTATO AND EGG SUPPER

4 strips bacon
4 C. diced cooked potatoes
6 hard-cooked eggs, sliced
1-10½ oz. can cream of
   chicken soup
1 C. milk

⅛ tsp. oregano
½ tsp. salt (onion)
¼ tsp. garlic salt
⅛ tsp. pepper
1 T. instant minced onion
1 C. shredded Cheddar
   cheese

Preheat oven to 375°. Fry bacon until crisp; crumble. Brush 2-quart casserole with bacon drippings. Layer potatoes, bacon, and eggs in casserole. Blend soup, milk, oregano, onion salt, garlic salt and onion; pour over potato mixture. Sprinkle cheese over top and bake 35 to 40 minutes. Makes 4 to 6 servings.

QUICK BACON-NOODLE CASSEROLE

2 C. noodles (¼ lb.)	1-#2 can tomatoes (2½ C.)
8 slices bacon, halved	1 C. fresh bread crumbs
¼ C. bacon fat	1½ tsp. salt
1 clove garlic, halved	1 tsp. sugar
½ C. minced onions	¼ C. Parmesan cheese

Preheat oven to 350°. Cook noodles as package directs; drain. Meanwhile, in skillet cook bacon until crisp; remove. Pour off bacon fat into a cup, then measure ¼ cup back in skillet. Add garlic; cook 2 or 3 minutes; remove. Add onions; cook until tender. Then add tomatoes, crumbs, salt, sugar and cheese. Cook 8 to 10 minutes. Pour into 1½-quart buttered casserole. Add noodles and bacon; toss well. Bake 30 minutes, covered. Makes 4 servings.

LIVER-BACON-POTATO CASSEROLE

1 lb. sliced bacon
2 medium onions, sliced
1 lb. liver (any kind), sliced
1 T. butter
1 T. flour
1 C. milk
1 tsp. prepared mustard

1 tsp. Worcestershire sauce
2 tsp. prepared horseradish
½ tsp. salt
⅛ tsp. pepper
1 lb. frozen hash browns
½ C. grated Cheddar
 cheese

Preheat oven to 350°. Cook bacon until crispy. Remove from skillet, drain and crumble. Pour off most of fat. Add onion to skillet and saute until golden. Push aside, add liver and cook until browned and done. Remove liver and cut into cubes. Melt butter in saucepan and blend in flour. Gradually add milk and cook, stirring, until thickened. Add next 5 ingredients. Put liver, bacon (1 cup), onion, and potato in bottom of 1½-quart casserole. Add sauce and mix well. Mix remaining bacon and cheese and sprinkle on top. Bake 30 minutes.

NOTE: If desired, 4 cups of cold diced, cooked potatoes can be substituted for hash browns. Makes 6 servings.

SUNDAY-DINNER CASSEROLE

1½ lbs. lean veal shoulder,
  cut in 1" cubes
1 C. chopped onion
1 tsp. salt
¼ tsp. pepper
½ tsp. MSG
2 C. water

½ lb. wide noodles
1-6 oz. can sliced
  mushrooms
½ pt. commercial sour
  cream
3 T. butter
1 C. fresh bread crumbs
¼ C. Parmesan cheese
¼ C. parsley, snipped

Preheat oven to 350°. Simmer veal with salt, pepper, monosodium glutamate, and water, covered, 1 hour or until very tender. Cook noodles in boiling salted water just 3 minutes; drain, then add to veal, with undrained mushrooms and sour cream. Test for seasoning. Put in 3-quart buttered casserole. Melt butter; stir in bread crumbs; remove from heat. Stir in cheese, parsley, sprinkle over mixture in 3-quart buttered casserole. Bake 1 hour, uncovered. Makes 8 servings.

SMOKED BEEF AND MACARONI

1-3½ oz. pkg. sliced,
  smoked beef, snipped
1-15 oz. can (2 C.) macaroni
  and cheese
1-3 oz. can chopped
  mushrooms, drained
2 oz. sharp Cheddar
  cheese, shredded

¼ C. chopped green pepper
1 hard-cooked egg, chopped
1 T. instant minced onion
½ tsp. Worcestershire sauce
½ C. bread crumbs
2 T. melted butter

Preheat oven to 350°. Combine all ingredients except crumbs and butter; put into greased 1-quart casserole. Combine crumbs and butter and put atop. Bake, uncovered, 35 to 40 minutes. Garnish with green pepper rings or hard-cooked egg slices if desired. Makes 4 servings.

MACARONI AND SAUSAGE CASSEROLE

1 lb. bulk sausage	2 C. milk
1 C. diced onion	2 C. macaroni, uncooked
1 C. diced green pepper	1 T. chili powder
2 C. tomatoes	1 tsp. salt

Preheat oven to 325 to 350°. Brown sausage, onion, and green pepper. Add tomatoes, milk, uncooked macaroni and seasonings. Cover in 2-quart buttered casserole dish and bake.

ITALIAN PORK-AND-RICE CASSEROLE

2 medium onions, sliced
1 clove garlic
2 T. oil
1-10¾ oz. can beef gravy
3-8 oz. cans tomato sauce
1-3 oz. can whole
  mushrooms, undrained
2 T. snipped parsley

1-3 lb. loin of pork, cut from
  bone in ¼" slices
¾ tsp. salt
¼ tsp. pepper
2 T. oil
2 C. raw rice
3 or 4 onions, sliced
3 green peppers, cut in
  eighths
½ tsp. salt

Preheat oven to 350°. In skillet, saute 2 onions and garlic in 2 tablespoons oil until golden brown; discard garlic. Add gravy, tomato sauce, mushrooms and parsley. Simmer, uncovered, 1 hour. Sprinkle pork with $\frac{3}{4}$ teaspoon salt and $\frac{1}{4}$ teaspoon pepper; saute in skillet in 2 tablespoons oil until brown all over. Remove pork. To drippings in pan add a little tomato gravy; stir to dissolve meat particles; add rest of the gravy. In 3-quart buttered casserole, arrange half of pork slices, top with rice combined with half the gravy. Add half of remaining onions, rest of pork. Cover with the other half of onions, then peppers. Pour on rest of gravy and bake $1\frac{1}{2}$ hours. Makes 8 servings.

MEXICAN SUPPER CASSEROLE

¼ C. chopped onion
¼ C. chopped green pepper
1 T. butter
2-15 oz. cans chili with beans
1-12 oz. can whole kernel
  corn, drained

1-4½ oz. can chopped ripe
  olives
1-4 oz. pkg. shredded sharp
  Cheddar cheese
1 pkg. corn muffin mix

Preheat oven to 400°. In large skillet, cook onion and pepper in butter until tender. Stir in chili, corn, and olives; bring to boiling. Add cheese, stir to melt. Put into greased 11x7x2½" baking pan. Prepare muffin mix according to package directions. Spoon dough in diagonal bands across top of casserole. Bake 15 to 20 minutes. Makes 8 servings.

UNI-Cookbook Categories

1100	Cookies	3400	Low Cholesterol
1200	Casseroles	3500	Chocoholic
1300	Meat Dishes	3700	Cajun
1400	Microwave	3800	Household Hints
1500	Cooking for "2"	6100	Chinese Recipes
1600	Slow Cooking	6400	German Recipes
1700	Low Calorie	6700	Italian Recipes
1900	Pastries & Pies	6800	Irish Recipes
2000	Charcoal Grilling	7000	Mexican Recipes
2100	Hors D'oeuvres	7100	Norwegian Recipes
2200	Beef	7200	Swedish Recipes
2300	Holiday Collections		
2400	Salads & Dressings		
2500	How to Cook Wild Game		
2600	Soups		
3100	Seafood & Fish		
3200	Poultry		
3300	My Own Recipes		

Available Titles 1/94

Titles change without notice.

G&R Publishing Co.
507 Industrial Street
Waverly, IA 50677